CONTENTS

THIS BOOK: 4

THE ANCIENT WORLD: 6
Build a Civilization ... from mud 8
Remember Your Cat ...
by making it a mummy 10
Base a Philosophy ... on beans 12
Mint Your Own Money ... from sand 14
Make a God ... out of your pet 16
Learn the Future ...
from a hole in the ground 18

THE MIDDLE AGES: 20
Become a Queen ...
by leaving the king 22
Start a Democracy ... with wet feet 24
Win Battles ...
by shooting backwards 26
Free the Peasants ...
by starting the Plague 28
Become Filthy Rich ...
by preaching poverty 30
Make a Textile Industry ...
with a walking stick 32
Make Money Worthless ...
by going on a pilgrimage 34
Run an Empire ... with a ball of string 36
Destroy a Country ...
by making statues 38

THE EARLY MODERN WORLD: 40
Become a Saint ... by going to war 42
Start a Renaissance ...
by getting naked 44
Discover a Continent ...
by going the wrong way 46
Destroy an Empire ...
with 16 horses 48
Buy an Island ... with peanuts 50

Destroy a City ...
with a loaf of bread 52
Modernize a Country ...
by having a shave 54
Get Rid of a Rubbish King ...
with an axe 56
Settle a New Continent ...
by getting rid of convicts 58
Lose an Empire ... over a cup of tea 60

INDUSTRY AND EMPIRE: 62
Create a Land of the Free ...
with slave labour 64
Start an Industrial Revolution ...
with a kettle 66
Conquer Africa ... with a piece of wood 68
Defeat a Killer Disease ... with a map 70
Turn Science on its Head ...
with a chaffinch 72
Abolish Slavery ... with a story book 74
Share Out a Desert ... with a ruler 76

THE MODERN WORLD 78
Fight a War ... by sitting still 80
Win the Vote ... with an iron chain 82
Get Out of a Depression ...
by planting trees 84
Invent Modern Art ...
by spilling some paint 86
Go to the Moon ...
with a pocket calculator 88
Become President ... by being an actor 90
Talk to the World ... with a mouse 92

Cool Words 94

Find Out More 95

Index 96

THIS BOOK

This book is about the past. The past includes everything from the beginning of time to right now. That's a long time (and it's getting longer). We try to make sense of it by turning it into 'history'.

History is kind of the same as the past – but kind of not. The past was a huge jumble of stuff that happened to different people at different times. History sorts the past into stories with beginnings and ends, even though people at the time weren't aware that they were part of a story. History tries to work out what was (important) and what wasn't. It usually stars people who changed the world around them in some way – not people who just stayed at home and played computer games to pass the time.

For example, the fact that you had toast for breakfast is definitely the past – but it's not really history.

Good and bad history

History makes the past look a lot more sensible than it really was. It tells a story of how everything started out a bit rubbish (the olden days) and then gradually got better until we got to today, with democracy and freedom of speech and books and travel and medicine and great movies and the Internet and everything.

As well as books about history, of course, plenty of books are PART of history. Take the Bible, for example, or the Koran. Look at pages 74-75 for a famous example.

HOW TO CHANGE THE WORLD WITH A BALL OF STRING

WARNING GRIPPING!

1776

History makes it look as though everyone knew what they were doing all along. In fact, it wasn't like that at all. Stuff happened by accident or had the opposite result from what was intended. That's what *How to Change the World with a Ball of String* is about … times when history wasn't very sensible.

The book has five chapters. They're kind of chronological, though they overlap a bit at the edges (because historical periods never start and finish exactly). You can read them in any order.

This book uses the abbreviations BCE and CE. BCE stands for 'before the Common Era'; it refers to the period before the year 0 CE, or 'Common Era', refers to dates since the year 0.

1521

1829

History contains all sorts – so look out for science, warfare, art, religion, exploration, more warfare, economics, politics, yet more warfare, ideas, animals and revolution. (Oh, and don't forget the warfare!)

You probably know that history has lots of grisly bits. Don't worry, we've left them all in (but be warned... you won't BELIEVE what the Egyptians did to their pets; check out pages 10–11).

THE ANCIENT WORLD

In the dim and distant past, things were often a bit, er ... dim and distant. This chapter MIGHT make things a bit clearer about the ancient Egyptians, Greeks and Romans. They had a bit more of a clue about what they were doing than you might think.

480 BCE

I know the future, you know ...

BUILD A CIVILIZATION ...
FROM MUD

CAST LIST

- Mud
- Sunshine
- Builders
- Town planners

The first great civilization of the Middle East achieved many things, including inventing writing. But its roots lay in the dirt ... literally.

Agriculture was another achievement of Mesopotamia, Greek for 'between the rivers'. The region lies between the Tigris and Euphrates, which meet north of the Persian Gulf. Regular floods deposited rich silt on the plain between the rivers, so it was perfect for growing crops. In about 5000 BCE, people could for the first time settle in one place and grow crops. They developed plants that produced more food. The most important were cereals such as wheat and barley that were ground into flour and baked into bread.

Mud, glorious mud

The river mud had another use, too. Earlier humans had lived in caves or in huts made from reeds or wood. A settled people could build not just permanent homes, but whole cities.

Bread had so much grit in that it ground down everyone's teeth.

Little HISTORY

c.3500 BCE: The wheel is invented in Mesopotamia

c.3200 BCE: The Sumerians make bronze

c.3000 BCE: Sumerian city-states emerge in Mesopotamia (now Iraq)

c.2200 BCE: The Sumerians introduce the calendar

c.2100 BCE: Sumerians build the first ziggurats

ACHIEVEMENTS OF SUMER

Sumer was one of the first civilizations – but it was pretty advanced. These are just some of the things that the Sumerians invented before anyone else.

- Writing
- Calendar
- Mathematics
- Fired pottery
- Weaving
- Wheel
- Bricks

Build a
ZIGGURAT

WHAT YOU'LL NEED

water
earth
wood moulds

1. Use pieces of wood to make a square mould about the size of a brick.

2. Put the mould on a flat surface and fill it with mud.

3. Put the mould in a sunny place (you may want to do this BEFORE it's full of runny mud).

4. Leave to dry. After a couple of days, lift off the mould to reveal your brick.

5. Repeat about 10 million times (for a medium-sized ziggurat).

6. Arrange the bricks in up to seven square layers, each a little smaller than the one below.

(OR you could just make a mini-ziggurat out of building blocks – you won't need so many and it won't take up so much of your bedroom.)

WARNING! DIRTY HANDS!

SQUELCH!

The Mesopotamians built with bricks. They tipped mud mixed with straw into moulds and left the bricks to bake hard in the sun. With millions of bricks, the Mesopotamians built cities like Ur and Nippur. Sumer emerged as the dominant power. The Sumerians built step-sided pyramids called ziggurats as temples to their gods. Bricks also formed huge walls to defend cities from their neighbours: there were frequent wars.

A ziggurat may have inspired the story of the Tower of Babel in the Bible.

Dust to dust

Sumer flourished for around 3,000 years – until another power took its place: Babylon. By then great cities stood all over the Mesopotamian plain. In the end, however, the rivers changed course and the climate changed. Everything got drier. Slowly the cities were abandoned and the bricks began to wear back to dust.

REMEMBER YOUR CAT ...
BY MAKING IT A MUMMY

Did you know that the ancient Egyptians turned their cats into mummies too? And not to catch rats and mice in the Underworld.

The town of Bubastis was sacred to the goddess Bastet, whom the Egyptians worshipped in the form of ... a cat. So the townspeople kept the goddess happy with suitable offerings: thousands upon thousands of cat mummies buried in vast cemeteries. The cats were bred to be (sacrificed) Bastet's priests broke kittens' necks – hundreds a day. It wasn't a job for the squeamish.

WARNING: gruesome bit coming up – pet lovers stop reading NOW!

Danger zone

It wasn't just cats. The Egyptians often imagined their gods as animals or as people with animals' heads. They made offerings to them all. That made Egypt dangerous for most kinds of animal: hawks, baboons, jackals, crocodiles and hippos. Even lizards and beetles were mummified.

Maybe I should leave the country...

CAST LIST

- Dead animals x millions
- Gods with animal heads

Little HISTORY

c.3300 BCE: First Egyptian mummies
c.900 BCE: Cats are mummified after they die
c.332 BCE: Animals are raised just to be sacrificed
c.30 BCE: Animal mummies die out (geddit?)

Mummify your PET

WHAT YOU'LL NEED

A pet
Bandages

CENSORED

MUMMY!!!

1 Grab your pet and ▓▓▓▓ (▓▓▓▓▓▓▓▓).
2 ▓▓▓▓ your pet ▓▓▓▓ ▓▓▓▓▓▓, ▓▓▓▓ brains through its nose.
3 ▓▓▓▓▓▓▓ to ▓▓▓▓ ▓▓▓▓ ▓▓▓▓▓▓▓.
4 Take a ▓▓▓▓ ▓▓▓▓ ▓▓▓▓▓▓. ▓▓▓ out of its bottom.
5 Pack ▓▓▓▓▓ to dry out. **CENSORED**
6 ▓▓▓ ▓▓▓▓▓ bandages.
7 Take your mummy to school to show your friends.

WARNING! DON'T TRY THIS AT HOME!

Mmm ... organs

Making an animal mummy was like making a human mummy. First the organs were removed (usually through the animal's bottom). Then the body was packed in a chemical called natron to dry it out. The dried body was wrapped in bandages – though not in fine linen, like royal mummies.

That pet's past it

Some pets were made into mummies, too. Monkeys and dogs were buried to keep their owners company. The Egyptians thought that the Afterlife was like this world, so they wanted to take their pets with them. Admittedly, it was a bit unlucky for pets to be killed just because their owners died – although some did get to live out their natural lives before they were put in their owners' tombs. (And anyway, perhaps they had loads of fun playing with their owners in the Afterlife.)

BASE A PHILOSOPHY ...
ON BEANS

The ancient Greek Pythagoras is famous as one of the greatest philosophers and mathematicians who ever lived – but he had some odd ideas about vegetables.

To be exact, Pythagoras's problem was actually with pulses. He warned his followers not to eat beans. No one knows exactly why. In the past 2,500 years many of his teachings have been lost or have changed completely. He believed in the soul, and may have banned his disciples from eating animals because they possessed souls. Some people wonder if he may have believed that beans had souls, too. Or perhaps he was just worried that they would give everyone too much wind.

Smart move

Pythagoras was smarter when it came to other stuff. In particular he gets credit for discoveries in mathematics and music that are still impressive today. They include the (theorem) named after him.

Some historians think Pythagoras didn't actually invent his own theorem: it may have been created by his followers.

Where did I put my keys?

WHO WAS WHO?

Pythagoras (c.580–c.500 BCE)

No one knows much about Pythagoras (although we do know that he probably wasn't a god, as his disciples said). He came from Samos in Greece, but moved to Italy in about 532 BCE because his religious ideas were unpopular in Greece. In Italy he set up a famous academy to teach his beliefs.

CAST LIST

- Brainy Greek
- Beans
- Right-angled triangles

Cult figure

In his own lifetime, Pythagoras was mainly famous as a philosopher who had a lot of ideas about gods and faith. He started a religious cult in the Greek colony of Croton, in what is now southern Italy. There were stories that he was a god himself. People said that he appeared in more than one place at the same time, and that his thigh was made of gold. Pythagoras taught that reality is based on order. At a deep level, he said everything could be explained by maths. The relationships between everything were based on harmony and balance, like music. He also argued that the human soul (and maybe a bean's soul) became united with a divine being after death. That became a very important idea for later religions, such as Christianity.

WARNING DEEP IN THOUGHT!

Copycats!

Pythagoras lived at the start of a golden age for Greek philosophy. He influenced later thinkers such as Plato and Aristotle. Through them, his ideas remained influential for thousands of years. People still read the works of the Greek philosophers today.

PYTHAGORAS'S THEOREM

This famous law says that the area of a square drawn on the longest side (or hypotenuse) of a right-angled triangle is equal to the sum of squares drawn on the other two sides. It's often used to calculate lengths and areas.

A

C

hypotenuse

right-angled triangle

B

Little HISTORY

c.532 BCE: Pythagoras moves to Italy to start an academy

c.380 BCE: Plato forms an academy

367 BCE: Aristotle begins 20 years at Plato's academy

MINT YOUR OWN MONEY ...
FROM SAND

In the story, King Midas is famous for his golden touch. The myth had some truth – the region where he lived was the first place to make its own coins.

In the ancient world people exchanged goods for what they needed. A farmer might swap corn for some fish from a fisherman, for example. But as communities grew more complex, it became important to have a different way to trade: money.

The first gold coins were probably minted in the kingdom of Lydia in Anatolia in the middle of what is now Turkey between 560 and 546 BCE. The Lydian king's wealth was famous. Even today we still have a phrase that uses his name to describe someone wealthy: 'As rich as Croesus'.

Gold was so rare that it was very valuable. Its colour reminded people of the sun, so it was ideal for making offerings to the gods.

MONEY! MONEY! MONEY!

Pan for GOLD

WHAT YOU'LL NEED
Sandy river with clean water
Fine sieve

1 Scoop up some sand from the river bed in your sieve.
2 Hold the sieve in the current to wash away the light sand.
3 Tilt the sieve so heavier grit sinks to the bottom; wash away the light grit.
4 Look in the grit left in the sieve for shiny specks – gold!
5 Be careful not to drop the gold dust, or you'll have to start again.

When the past was RUBBISH

This money won't fit my pocket

The Pacific island of Yap had its own money – but you wouldn't want it for pocket money! Their 'coins' were discs of rock with holes cut in the middle. Some were twice as tall as a man; even medium-sized ones were too heavy to carry. The islanders only used them for special occasions. Eventually, they stopped even moving the rocks … they just remembered who owned which one.

Coining it

Croesus's early coins were made from electrum, a natural alloy of gold and silver. The mineral came from the River Pactolus, which flowed through Lydia. The coins weren't like modern coins. They were very small and not very round. Because they were beaten flat with a hammer, they were only rough circles. But they did have a lion and a bull stamped on them to show that they were official currency.

Later, Croesus began making two types of coins: silver and gold.

Goldfinger

A famous myth that explained the gold in the river was based on a real king of the 8th century BCE. Midas wished that everything he touched would turn to gold. Midas soon realized that his gift was a curse – so he washed off his golden touch in the Pactolus. From then on, the river's sand was full of gold.

Even his daughter turned into a golden statue when he hugged her.

CAST LIST

- Midas
- Croesus
- Special river
- Electrum

Little HISTORY

c.700 BCE: Silver coins made in Argos, Greece.

c.740 BCE: King Mita (Midas) dies in Phrygia.

c.560 BCE: Croesus becomes king of Lydia

c.550 BCE: First gold coins made by Croesus.

15

MAKE A GOD ...
OUT OF YOUR PET

Everyone worships their pets, right? But for most people that doesn't mean that you *actually* worship them. Unless, of course, you're a Roman emperor ... and you're a bit crazy.

Caligula didn't start off crazy. When he became emperor in 37 CE, he was quite sane. After the death of his father Germanicus – a very popular Roman general – the boy had been brought up by his great-uncle, the emperor Tiberius. (The boy's name was actually Gaius: Caligula was a nickname given to him by soldiers when the child accompanied his father on campaign; it meant 'little boots'.)

Tiberius had killed the rest of Caligula's family to prevent any challenge to his rule.

WARNING NASTY BITE!

Odd Gods
• Cats (ancient Egypt)
• Cobras (some Hindus)
• The Duke of Edinburgh (Yaohnanen tribe, Vanuatu)

CAST LIST
• Mad emperor
• Crazy horse
• Golden oats

16

Make your own GOD

WHAT YOU'LL NEED

A pet
Disciples

1 Dress your pet in something godlike (i.e. a halo).

2 Give your pet a good god's name, like Thor or Jupiter.

3 Start praying to your pet where people can see you. Carry on until they join in. (If they don't, quietly stop and try with another pet.)

Mad, bad and dangerous

To begin with, Caligula ruled well. Then something changed: he went a little bonkers. He spent huge amounts on new palaces. He used boats to build a floating bridge 3 kilometres long. He once fed lots of people to the lions in the arena because he was bored. (They had only come to watch!) He marched his army north to invade Britain ... but when they reached the coast of France, he ordered them to collect seashells instead. And he tried to make his horse, Incitatus, a consul and a priest (OK – it's not really a god, but it's close enough). He fed Incitatus oats mixed with flakes of gold. Caligula made his dead sister a god and tried to make himself a god. He dressed as a god, and put his own bust on top of statues of the gods.

Done to death

It's hard to tell if all the stories about Caligula are true. Lots of the people who wrote them down were his enemies. But he does seem to have been crazy, even compared to other Roman emperors (a lot of whom were barking mad). He was bad enough for the Romans to get rid of him – he was stabbed by his own guards in 41 CE.

WOOF!

Little HISTORY

37 CE: Becomes emperor

38: Programme of political reform

39: Builds a floating bridge

40: Claims to be a god

41: Stabbed to death

LEARN THE FUTURE ...
FROM A HOLE IN THE GROUND

Being Apollo's priestess was an easy job: you only worked one day a month. But you did have to pass on the god's messages ... and hang out in a cave.

CAST LIST

- Apollo (the god, not the rocket)
- Priestess
- Gas

The Greeks thought that the gods were like humans. They lived in families, they partied ... and they quarrelled. The last thing anyone wanted to do was to irritate a moody god. So before the Greeks did anything – anything important, anyway – they found out what the gods wanted them to do.

There were different ways to find that out. You could, say, kill an animal, pull out its insides and interpret any marks on its liver (not very accurate – and VERY messy). Instead most Greeks consulted an oracle – a person through whom a god or goddess spoke. To get in touch with Apollo, you had to head to Delphi, in the mountains of central Greece.

Apollo was god of the sun, medicine, fortune telling, music, poetry, art ... and more. Phew!

Little HISTORY

650 BCE: Apollo's cult is well established

c.547 BCE: Croesus consults the oracle

c.480 BCE: Athenians and Spartans consult the oracle

393 CE: Last response of the oracle

PHEW!! SMELLY!

Snake tongue

Delphi attracted people from all over Greece. It stood in a place where two hills met to form a ravine with a sacred spring. Apollo had once killed a monster serpent there, so the oracle who gave his messages was called the Pythia (or 'python').

She was a priestess who sat in a cave on a special three-legged seat. The god's breath – gases from a hole under the seat – entered her and came out of her mouth as words or noises. (Priests translated the noises into words.) The oracle only prophesied on the seventh day of each month, because seven was Apollo's lucky number.

A shrine grew up as rich people built temples after taking the oracle's advice.

A load of hot air

The problem was, it was difficult to interpret the oracle's predictions. She was famous for the fact that her words could mean nearly anything. When the Lydian king Croesus asked her if he should go to war against the Persians, she said that if he went to war he would bring down a mighty empire. Croesus assumed she meant Persia and attacked ... only to discover too late that the mighty empire he would destroy was his own. Whoops!

Er ... well ... yes ... and no!

She advised the Athenians to protect themselves with 'wooden walls' – they guessed she meant ships.

WARNING GAS ATTACK!

When the past was RUBBISH

For sooth's sake

Ancient cultures spent a lot of time trying to predict the future. Oracles were common: dreams were also thought to contain clues about what was going to happen. In ancient China, soothsayers (fortune tellers) heated turtle shells and interpreted the cracks that appeared. The study of animal entrails, or haruscipation, was another favourite. Today, of course, millions of people study their horoscopes to find out the influence of the planets – a method first used by the ancient Babylonians over 3,500 years ago.

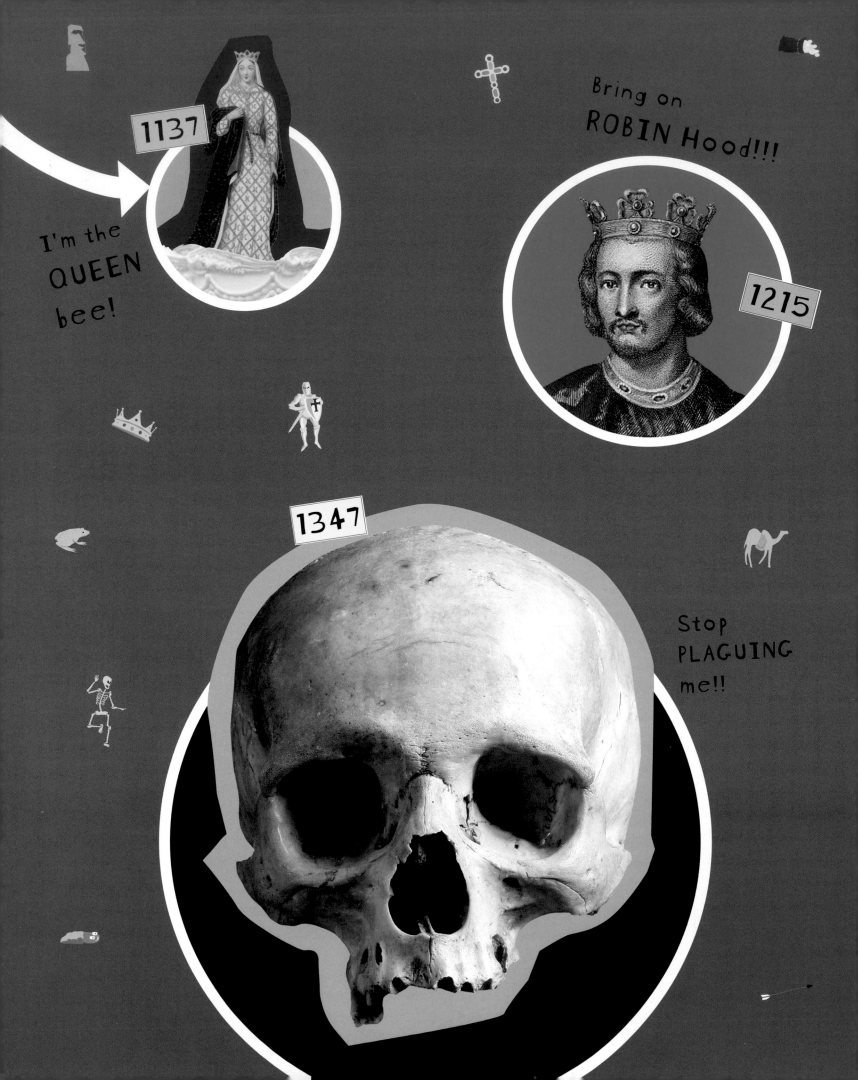

THE MIDDLE AGES

The Middle Ages used to be known as the Dark Ages. In fact, they were pretty illuminated (well, maybe not at night). They started when the Roman Empire fell in 476 and lasted until about 1453, when the Turks captured Constantinople.

Llazy llama

1493

1492

Ker-ching!

BECOME A QUEEN ...
BY LEAVING THE KING

Eleanor of Aquitaine was no ordinary woman. For one thing, she was a duchess. For another, she married twice ... and was queen of two countries.

Eleanor seemed a bit too flighty to become the most powerful woman in 12th-century Europe. But she was used to power and inherited a huge domain – so it was no real surprise that she married a prince, Louis, who became king of France in 1137.

Louis VII adored his wife... until he took her with him on a crusade to the Holy Land. She soon began to upset him. She was such close friends with her uncle, Raymond of Poitiers, that Louis had to kidnap her to make sure she stayed with his forces in Jerusalem, not Raymond's in nearby Antioch. When it was time to return to Europe, the pair weren't talking. They sailed on different boats. At home, even the Pope tried to get them to make up. In the end, they were divorced in 1152 (this was at a time when very few people got divorced).

The church said that Eleanor was too extravagant.

COURTLY COURT

In the 1170s, Eleanor made her palace at Poitiers a centre of chivalry. The tradition of 'courtly love' set out rules about how knights should act. A knight should be in love with a woman, for example, but only from a distance. In reality, of course, knights were rough and violent, but under Eleanor's influence the idea of courtly love became popular. It inspired many of the famous tales of King Arthur and his knights of the Round Table.

CAST LIST

- Rich duchess
- King I
- King II

22

NEXT!

Henry was a toy boy – he was 12 years younger than Eleanor.

Single again

Eleanor still owned Aquitaine – so she became the most eligible bride in Europe. Two French lords tried to kidnap and marry her. In the end she chose (Henry) Plantagenet, duke of Normandy – and a grandson of the English king. In 1154 he became King Henry II of England, uniting England, Normandy and western France.

Now, now, boys ...

Eleanor was very involved in politics ... maybe too closely. When her sons tried to overthrow Henry in 1173, the queen was blamed. She was shut up at home until Henry died in 1189. Eleanor's son became King Richard I (the Lionheart). While he was away fighting in the Crusades, she ran the kingdom. When Richard died, another of her sons became King John I. Eleanor carefully arranged marriages to ensure that the French and the English remained friendly – even though by then she was over 80 ... and probably fancied a rest!

Little HISTORY

1137: Queen of France
1152: Divorced
1154: Queen of England
1173: Imprisoned
1189: Regent for Richard I
1204: Dies

Nun Better!

Eleanor ended her life in a convent. When she died, the nuns said that 'she was beautiful and just, imposing and modest, humble and elegant'. They said that she 'surpassed almost all of the queens in the world' (which kind of makes you wonder which queens she didn't surpass).

WHO WAS WHO?

Richard the Lionheart (1157–1199)

Richard the Lionheart is famous from the Robin Hood stories. He was the 'good' king, whose 'bad' brother Prince John tried to steal his throne while Richard was at the Crusades. Richard is an unlikely British hero. He didn't like Britain – he complained that it was too rainy and only spent six months of his 10-year reign there, preferring to live in his French duchy of Aquitaine. He couldn't even speak English. But he had a popular reputation as a brave warrior who fought for Christianity against the Muslims.

START A DEMOCRACY ...
WITH WET FEET

Medieval kings were, er, king pins. They could do what they wanted. Until, that is, the English put their feet down (squelch).

King John of England was so unpopular with his subjects that in 1215 the most powerful barons in the kingdom rebelled and marched on London. If they could have decided who to put on the throne instead, they might have overthrown John. As it was, they came to an agreement with him. On 15 June, 1215, the king and some 62 barons met at Runnymede, on the River Thames west of London, in a water meadow (a field kept purposely damp for growing crops).

The Londoners opened their gates to the rebels – they didn't think much of John, either.

WHO WAS WHO?

King John I (1167–1216)

John I was a bad king. He failed to capture Robin Hood. He had to back down in a dispute with the Pope. He was no good at fighting, which was useless for a king. He lost to the French. When he was losing to the barons, the French invaded and he started losing to them again. He ran away, but lost the crown jewels in an ocean marsh when the tide came in. The shock helped to kill him a couple of days later.

Little HISTORY

- **1215:** John agrees Magna Carta
- **1216:** John dies
- **1225:** Charter becomes law under Henry III
- **1297:** Edward I reissues Charter in return for setting a new tax

CROAK!

Magna Carta

Magna Carta (the name just means 'great charter') was a key document for individual freedom. It protected citizens from their rulers. It was also a step towards the principle that a government could only rule with the consent of the citizens.

Blinking barons!

The barons had prepared a (document) setting out limits on the king's power. A new committee – made up of barons, of course – would be able to overrule the king if he ignored the charter. John agreed and stamped his seal on the document. But as soon as the barons left London, he abandoned it (everyone knew he (would)). The barons and John began a civil war … but then the king suddenly died.

It was based on the Charter of Liberties granted by Henry I in 1100.

Starta the Carta

John's death saved Magna Carta. It became law under his son, Henry III, in 1225. It was reissued in 1297 – and it is still part of English and Welsh law. It was important for setting the limits of the king's power. It also guaranteed citizens' freedoms, such as the protection of the law of the land. No one could be punished just because the king (or anyone else for that matter) felt like it.

That's what kings did: even the Pope was on John's side.

WIN BATTLES ...
BY SHOOTING BACKWARDS

In the 13th century the Mongols of central Asia built the biggest empire in the world ... thanks to a brilliantly simple invention.

In 1206 a leader named Temujin united all the tribes who lived a nomadic existence on the great plains of Mongolia. Temujin took a new name: Genghis Khan, or 'great leader'. Within two decades, that name would strike fear into people across the whole of Asia. Under Genghis, the Mongols began a campaign of conquest that would create the greatest contiguous empire the world has ever seen.

contiguous means joined together, not scattered like, say, the British empire.

TWANG!

I THINK HE'LL GET THE POINT!

Little HISTORY

1206: Genghis Khan unites the Mongols

1220: Asia conquered

1234: China conquered

1241: Italy invaded

1312: Last Mongol invasion, of Syria

Gee up Neddy!

Genghis reorganized the Mongol army based on units of 10, 100, 1,000 and 10,000. The Mongols were expert riders – their lifestyle was based on horses – so most of their army was made up of (cavalry.) They could advance up to 160 kilometres a day by swapping horses to keep them fresh. In battle, mounted archers fired a hail of arrows before mounted lancers finished off the enemy.

The Mongols didn't lose a battle until 1260 – to an army that copied Mongol tactics!

Foot loose, fancy free

The Mongol cavalry were fast because they wore only light armour. They were also able to shoot arrows in all directions – even backwards – thanks to their stirrups. These cradles held their feet in place, so they had a solid base to shoot from (they also waited to fire until the horse's hoofs were all off the ground, which was the least bumpy part of riding along).

TRY THIS

Shoot arrows BACKWARDS

WHAT YOU'LL NEED
suction-cup arrows
bow   ruler   target

1 Put the target against a wall (with nothing breakable near it!).
2 Put the ruler on the floor about 2 metres from the target.
3 Stand with your toes against the ruler and your back to the target.
4 Keeping your toes against the ruler, twist at the waist to fire at the target. (You could try pretending to be on a horse by bouncing up and down when you shoot.)

WHO WAS WHO?

Genghis Khan (c.1162–1227)

Genghis Khan united the Mongols in 1206 and built an empire. His Mongol armies conquered much of central Asia and China. He was notorious for cruelty, including massacring conquered peoples. After his death, his heirs expanded the empire, which eventually covered a fifth of the Earth.

WARNING RAIN OF ARROWS!

FREE THE PEASANTS ...
BY STARTING THE PLAGUE

Being a peasant in medieval Europe was not much fun. You never went anywhere new. You couldn't even marry without your lord's permission.

Everyone who lived on the lord's land had a duty to work for him and to obey his instructions. In return, the (lord) had a responsibility to make sure they had a home and food to eat. This system of duties and responsibilities was known as feudalism. It worked well for everyone … according to the lords who got the most out of it. For peasants, things weren't quite so good. A few left the countryside to work in the growing towns. But most people's lives were always the same. No matter how clever they were or how hard they worked, the feudal system didn't allow them to change very much.

Lords had a duty to obey more important lords and so on, right up to the King.

Little HISTORY

1347: Black Death reaches Europe

1348: Reaches Italy, Spain, France and England

1349: Reaches Germany and the Low Countries

1350: Reaches Scandinavia

1350: Black Death dies out

Every cloud ...

Then in 1347 ships docked in Italy and southern France from the Crimea, Russia. Like all ships, they had loads of rats. But these rats carried fleas infected with a fatal disease known as the plague or the Black Death. Most victims died within two to seven days. In three years, the disease swept across Europe. The continent's population fell by about one-third.

Some 25 million people died, from geniuses and kings to mums, dads and children. There weren't enough people left to plant or harvest crops. Lots of farmland was abandoned.

... has a silver lining

Survivors of the Black Death found themselves very popular. Landlords wanted them to work in the fields, while there was loads of work in the towns. To get new recruits, employers were willing to pay – cash. Workers could demand high wages. In one blow, a modern economy had destroyed the feudal system.

- 25 million victims
- Bacteria on fleas
- Fleas on rats
- Rats

YOU DON'T LOOK SO GOOD!

WARNING DEAD HEAD!

When the past was RUBBISH

Can I have this dance?

After the Black Death, Europeans grew obsessed with death (not surprising, really!). The Dance of Death appeared in art. It showed a line of skeletons from all levels of society jiving to the grave. The message was clear: No matter who you were, in the end you had to do the dance!

R.I.P. 1348

BECOME FILTHY RICH ...
BY PREACHING POVERTY

Jesus said 'It is easier for a camel to pass through the eye of a needle than for a rich man to enter the kingdom of heaven.' So how come medieval priests lived like princes?

The message of the Bible was clear: wealth would not help anyone go to Heaven (and might even guarantee the opposite). That was a popular message. But by the Middle Ages, the church had become very powerful. Its spectacular buildings were full of valuable paintings and sculptures. Rich patrons paid for artworks or chapels in order to gain God's favour. Even peasants gave one-tenth of their crop – a tax called a tithe – to pay for a priest.

Most people were poor, so they liked the idea that the next world would be fairer than this one.

CAST LIST

- Greedy priests
- Corrupt popes
- Monks & nuns
- Protestants

Little HISTORY

517: First indulgences
1492: Alexander VI becomes pope
1517: Reformation begins

Indulgences

One way the church raised money was by selling 'indulgences'. These certificates were supposed to offer people a quicker way to Heaven after they died. They helped pay to build St. Peter's Church in Rome ... and sparked the protests that led to the Reformation.

Luxury living

The church was the richest institution in medieval Europe. The (popes) and cardinals who ran it lived like royal princes. Some of them got their jobs because they were from rich and powerful families, like the Borgias of Florence. Some were far more concerned with their own comfort than the spiritual well-being of their congregations.

Alexander VI (pope 1492–1503) had dozens of mistresses and children and sold off positions for cardinals.

Money makes the world

Small groups of ordinary people tried to return to the spirit of the Bible. They gave up their worldly possessions (of course, most people thought that was a bit weird). But in the end the row about wealth split the whole church. In the Reformation, which began in 1517, the protestors who left the church (Protestants, geddit?!) objected to the way rich people seemed to be able to buy their way into Heaven.

GREEDY!!

MONKS AND NUNS

Even in the 3rd century, some Christians thought that the power of the church contradicted Christ's teachings. Some people in Egypt and Syria moved to the desert to follow simple lives that echoed how Jesus had actually lived. They were the first monks and nuns. By the early Middle Ages, great monasteries grew up where monks continued to live simple lives of poverty.

31

MAKE A TEXTILE INDUSTRY ...
WITH A WALKING STICK

Leave some silkworms to spin cocoons, boil them ... and unravel your silk. Easy – if you know how (and you've got some silkworms).

CAST LIST

- Crooked monks
- Useless guards
- Handful of silkworms

For European fashionistas in the early Middle Ages, silk was to die for. Unlike most cloth of the time, it felt smooth and luxurious. It was expensive, though, which was hardly surprising as it came all the way from (Asia.) It was so valuable that Chinese rulers even used it to buy off nasty nomads who lived on their borders (obviously the nomads liked the odd luxury).

Ancient Greek and Roman weavers unwound Asian silk fabrics to make their own yarn.

Little HISTORY

c.2,500 BCE: Silk in China

c.140 BCE: Sericulture in India

c.550 CE: Sericulture in Europe

You can't be seri-ous

The Chinese claimed that sericulture (duh … making silk) had been introduced by the wife of the mythical Yellow Emperor, who founded Chinese culture in the 3rd millennium BCE. The secret lay in unwinding silkworm cocoons: each cocoon makes a kilometre of silk. The Chinese taught the secret to the Indians and Japanese – but no one else. It was too valuable to give away.

Oh, brother!

For Europeans, on the other hand, silk was too expensive to keep buying. In about 550 CE Emperor Justinian I of Byzantium sent two Persian monks to China to find the secret of silk. They came back with silkworms smuggled in their hollow bamboo walking sticks. Those few silkworms would become the basis of an industry that flourished in Europe, mainly in Italy and France, for about 1,300 years – the Chinese didn't get a look in (although most Europeans still couldn't afford the luxury of silk).

THE SILK ROAD

The Silk Road was a trade route across Central Asia that joined China in the east to the Roman empire in the west. Great cities grew up to act as staging posts on the way. Few people travelled the whole 4,600 kilometres: goods passed along from merchant to merchant. Ideas travelled, too. Buddhism and Islam both spread along the route before it declined in the 14th century.

When the past was RUBBISH

Get 'em off!

Governments used to spend a lot of time telling people what they could and couldn't do – including what they could wear. In the early Roman Empire, for example, men were banned from wearing silk. And in America in the 17th century only a man with a certain amount of money could wear lace (yes, I know … but in those days, lots of men actually *wanted* to wear lace). Shoes could only be so long and hats so high. Some colours or materials were forbidden to particular social classes. Governments said that such rules ensured that people didn't waste money. More often, it seemed that the rules just made sure that poorer people couldn't dress like the rich.

WARNING BOILED ALIVE!

33

MAKE MONEY WORTHLESS ...
BY GOING ON A PILGRIMAGE

The point of a pilgrimage is holy, of course. But Mansa Musa was no ordinary pilgrim ... so this was no ordinary pilgrimage.

'Mansa' means 'king of kings' or 'ruler of rulers' or 'emperor of emperors' – something big, anyway.

Musa (ruled) Mali in western Africa in the early 14th century. He was one of the richest men in the world, thanks to Mali's gold and its control of trade in the Sahara. Like all Muslims, Musa had a duty to visit Mecca in Arabia if he could – and it wasn't as if he couldn't afford it. So he set out in 1324, travelling in style. Musa was accompanied by 60,000 people: 12,000 of them were his own slaves, all wearing the finest Persian silk. Musa rode on a horse behind 500 slaves who all carried golden staffs.

WHO WAS WHO?

Mansa Musa (ruled c.1312–1337)

Musa was one of the most devout Muslims to rule Mali (not that it stopped him conquering the neighbouring Songhai empire). He built many holy buildings, including a great mosque in Timbuktu and a religious university at Sankoré (he also brought Muslim architects from Spain to build him a palace). Musa's fame was so great that European traders added Timbuktu to their maps – and plotted how to get hold of some of Mali's riches.

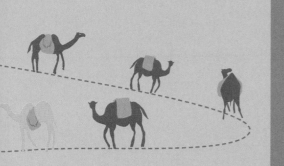

When the past was RUBBISH

Too much money

Too much money becomes worth a lot less. Some countries have tried printing money to get out of economic difficulty. It usually leads to disaster. In Germany in the 1920s prices doubled every two days until the currency was worthless; in Zimbabwe in the 2000s, inflation reached nearly 90 sextillion percent.

PHEW! THAT'S HEAVY!

Giving charity (zakat) is one of the basic duties of all Muslims.

All that glitters ...

As well as people, Musa had 80 camels, each carrying 135 kilograms of gold. Musa used it to buy supplies – he paid for everyone – and gave it away as gifts. One story claimed that each Friday, which is Islam's holy day, he didn't only pray in a mosque – he built a new mosque to pray in.

When Musa reached Cairo in Egypt, he spent so much gold on slaves and singing girls that it devalued the local currency. There was so much gold in the city that it wasn't worth anything. A decade later the Egyptian economy hadn't recovered. Even before he went home in 1325, though, Musa was broke. He had spent so much that he had to borrow money for his return journey.

The citizens of Cairo still remembered Musa's generosity, however.

CAST LIST
- Mansa Musa
- 60,000 Malians
- Some Egyptians
- Some Arabs

Little HISTORY

c.1312: Musa becomes Mansa
1324: Begins pilgrimage
1325: Returns home
1330: Loses but recaptures Timbuktu
1337: Last mention of Musa being alive

RUN AN EMPIRE ...
WITH A BALL OF STRING

It's hard enough to run a tuck shop without being able to keep records of orders and payments. Imagine trying to run a huge empire without any form of writing.

That's what the Inca of Peru did. They had no writing. They didn't even have the wheel. Their territory was divided by towering mountains with little room to grow crops. Most people would have spent their time growing corn and potatoes to survive. Not the Inca. From about 1100 until their downfall in 1532, they conquered other peoples and built the (largest empire) South America has ever seen. It stretched from what are now Chile and Argentina in the south to Ecuador in the north.

At its height in the 15th and 16th centuries, the Inca empire only lasted just over 100 years.

CAST LIST

- Inca (no one knows how many)
- Llamas (lots)
- A few Spaniards

LOVELY LLAMAS

The Inca might not have got far without the llama … literally. Llamas were the main beasts of burden, because the Inca had not invented the wheel (not that it would have been much use in the Andes, where everywhere is uphill). Llamas also provided wool and milk … and meat (of course the llama was not much use after that). Llamas were so important that the Inca made tiny golden llamas to offer to their gods.

Little
HISTORY

1100: Cusco founded
Pachacuti expands empire
Empire at its height
1532: Collapse of empire

Tied up in knots

The Inca ran things from their capital at Cusco. They built roads to take messengers throughout the empire – even over the high Andes. To govern such a wide area and to make sure people had enough to eat, the Inca kept careful records of population and food stores. But they didn't write them down. They kept them as quipu – knots tied into wool or string, which was gathered together in bundles.

The knots were a code … but after the Spaniards conquered the Inca in 1532 no one knew how to read them. Today we still have a few quipu – most were destroyed – but no one knows what they meant. (Perhaps they were full of jokes about llamas.)

Tie your own QUIPU

WHAT YOU'LL NEED

coloured string
scissors

paper and pencil

1. Work out a code and make a note of it. Combine a colour of string and a different number of knots for each letter.
2. Cut lengths of string about 10 centimetres long.
3. Tie knots in the string to spell out a message like 'The Incas were stinkers'.
4. Tie together the strings for each word into a bundle.
5. Tie all the bundles together at the top.
6. Challenge a friend to decode the meaning of the quipu.

Food for thought

The highlands of the Andes were useless for growing grain crops like wheat. The Inca's staple foods were corn and potatoes. Both came in many colours, including blue and black. They dug stepped terraces into the mountainsides to create more land to plant crops.

IT'S ALL UPHILL!

WARNING LIKES TO SPIT!

DESTROY A COUNTRY ...
BY MAKING STATUES

Basing a society on the idea of carving huge stone tributes to your ancestors doesn't allow much time to do anything else ... like making sure the society survives.

On a world map the size of this page, (Easter Island) would look like a pencil dot. It's a tiny place in the Pacific Ocean, about 3,500 kilometres from Chile. People settled there as late as 1200 CE. Maybe they wanted some peace and quiet ... they were 2,000 kilometres from their nearest neighbours. In around 1250 the islanders began to carve great stone heads, or *moai*. The tallest was 12 metres high. The statues were quarried, carved out of a block of stone and set up on stone platforms around the coast.

The island was named by a Dutch explorer who saw it on Easter Sunday 1722. Today it is known as Rapa Nui.

WARNING! DON'T SMOOCH THE STATUES!

Little HISTORY

c.1200: Easter Island settled

c.1250: First moai carved

c.1650: Last moai carved

c.1650: Trees disappear from island

1722: Europeans arrive

CAST
LIST
- Island
- Islanders
- Dead ancestors
- Big stones

Moving moai

Making the statues took a lot of effort. The moai were so large that quarrying, carving and transporting them needed help from everyone. The moai were probably moved to their final location using wooden rollers.

Some archaeologists think that the effort of making the statues eventually exhausted the islanders. The island's few trees were always being cut down to use as rollers or for firewood. By 1650 they had disappeared. The soil was poor for farming, but perhaps if people weren't so busy making statues they could have grown more food.

Meltdown!

Whatever happened, in the 17th century the society on Easter Island collapsed. By the time the Dutch arrived in 1722, the population had shrunk to a couple of thousand. The moai stood alone, gazing over their former territory…

People made smaller versions of moai to keep at home – they were far more portable than the 10-tonne giants.

WHAT WERE MOAI FOR?

The statues represented ancestors who were believed to help the living islanders. They were set up on their own or in rows on stone platforms named ahu. There are more than 800 statues (some are still in the quarry). Most stand around the edges of the island. They looked inland, as if they were watching over the islanders.

Vanished Civilizations

Around the world a number of ruins are evidence of the achievements of civilizations that disappeared completely.

- Tikal (Maya)
- Angkor (Khymer)
- Borobudur (Srivijaya)
- Machu Picchu (Inca)

Muscle man!

1413

1427

Allez France!

Is this the way to China?

1492

I wasn't that bad!

1792

THE EARLY MODERN WORLD

It's not really old but it's not quite modern: welcome to the Early Modern World. It lasted from the late Middle Ages to the start of the Industrial Revolution in the late 18th century (which is of course really QUITE modern).

1666

London's burning!

BECOME A SAINT ...
BY GOING TO WAR

Most saints are famous for being holy and peaceful. But the patron saint of France was a 15th-century peasant girl whose reputation is based on her fighting skills.

In the early 15th century the English king Henry V owned a duchy in southwestern France. When two families began to fight for the French throne in 1415, Henry invaded to try to win more territory. The invasion was just part of a long conflict between England and France now known as the Hundred Years' War.

In fact it lasted from 1337 to 1453: but the Hundred and Sixteen Years' War sounds a bit rubbish.

Henry and his allies won control of most of northern France. The French armies of Prince Charles were besieged in Orléans, in north-central France. It was the only major northern city still in French hands. If Orléans fell to the English, the rest of France might follow.

Pleasant peasant

Then Charles had an unexpected visit. A peasant girl claimed that God had told her to help defeat the English so that Charles could go to Reims in the northeast,

Little HISTORY

c.1412: Birth of Joan of Arc
1415: Henry V invades France
1427: Battle of Orléans
1429: Coronation of King Charles VII
1430: Joan captured in battle
1431: Joan executed at Rouen

- Girl with visions
- Ambitious prince
- The French (all of them!)

WARNING SHARP EDGE!

JOAN, YOU'RE AN ANGEL!

I've got a point to prove!

the city where French kings were usually crowned, for his coronation. Charles was impressed (he was also pretty desperate for some good news). He sent Joan on an expedition to Orléans to try to lift the siege.

Maid of Orléans

To everyone's surprise, Joan inspired a victory at Orléans. She led raids on English positions until the enemy withdrew. She became joint commander of the French army and led a campaign that ended with Charles being crowned in Reims. No one knows whether she was a tactical genius or a figurehead who gave the soldiers confidence. In May 1430 Joan was captured by the Burgundians and handed over to the English, who put her on trial. The English argued that Joan's visions did not come from God (of course, they believed God was on THEIR side). They put her on trial for heresy, or false religious beliefs. In reality, the 'Maid of Orléans' was such a heroine to the French that the English just wanted her out of the way. The court found her guilty and sentenced her to be burned to death. She died in the marketplace in Rouen on 30 May, 1431.

WHO WAS WHO?

Joan of Arc (c.1412–1431)

Joan was a farmer's daughter from Lorraine. She lived a holy life and claimed that God had told her to help Charles defeat the English. It was Joan's claim to be acting in the name of Christ that so infuriated the English. Even at her execution she still claimed to be guided by God. The Catholic Church made her a saint in 1920 – but for the French she had been a symbol of nationalism since soon after her death.

START A RENAISSANCE ...
BY GETTING NAKED

Artists like Leonardo da Vinci, Michelangelo, Raphael and Donatello are still world famous – and not only because of the teenage mutant ninja turtles.

Some of the greatest artists in history painted during the Renaissance. In the cities of Italy, Holland and Belgium painters followed new ways of thinking about the world. They were influenced by a philosophy called humanism which was based on ideas about, er, humans. This view saw individuals as being more important than earlier thinkers had thought ... and more interesting. Not surprisingly, such thinking was popular with Europe's new class of wealthy merchants, bankers and princes – they thought they were pretty important and interesting, too.

The Renaissance lasted from about 1250 to 1550.

In the Middle Ages, scholars saw the social order as being more important than individuals.

CAST LIST

- Curious artists
- Important patrons
- Dead bodies
- Nudists

You show off!

These Europeans did not want to be stuck in the Middle Ages. They looked back to the golden age of ancient Greece and Rome. They wanted to echo the ancient achievements. As part of this, they paid artists to paint portraits and classical scenes. The pictures were a way to show off their learning – and their wealth.

NO PEEKING!

Little HISTORY

1413: Appearance of perspective
1424: Masaccio paints *Expulsion from the Garden of Eden*
c.1504: Michelangelo sculpts *David*
c.1507: Leonardo paints *Mona Lisa*

That's really deep

Artists paid more attention to individuals, too. They studied naked figures (sometimes they even cut up dead bodies). They painted nudes in poses that showed off the muscles and tendons beneath the skin. In the early 15th century, for example, Masaccio painted Adam and Eve as real people, wailing as they are expelled from the Garden of Eden.

In 1413 the mathematician Filippo Brunelleschi developed the rules of perspective. It is a way of making a flat picture look as though it has depth, so some things look as if they are further away than others. It was a stunning change. Excited artists began to paint pictures with loads of lines so that they could show off their skill at perspective.

Leonardo's drawing of muscles in the arm and shoulder could only be done by cutting someone open!

WARNING ARTISTS WITH SAWS

TRY THIS

Draw your own PERSPECTIVE

WHAT YOU'LL NEED
paper
pencil
ruler
rubber
(because you WILL make mistakes)

1 Perspective is based on the idea that parallel lines seem to grow closer together as they recede to meet at an imaginary vanishing point on the horizon.
2 On your piece of paper draw a straight horizontal line to act as the horizon.
3 Draw a square in the bottom half of the paper.
4 Use a ruler to add sides to your square leading to a vanishing point on the horizon.
5 Adapt your cube to make more complex designs such as houses, with lines that all converge on the same vanishing point.

DISCOVER A CONTINENT ...
BY GOING THE WRONG WAY

LAND AHOY!

Europeans named the Americas 'the New World'. But the fact was, they didn't really want to go there in the first place.

It's the most famous wrong turn ever. In 1492 Christopher Columbus headed to the East Indies – which were, er, east – by sailing … west. That's right. Instead of sailing around Africa and east across the Indian Ocean, the plucky Italian reckoned there was a short cut around the globe west across the Atlantic.

Spices from the East Indies were worth a fortune (they made bad food taste OK). But the wrong way? No one was convinced … especially not the crew on his three ships. On the 34th day at sea they tried to turn back. Luckily for Columbus, two days later they saw land.

When the past was RUBBISH

Flat Earth society

In the 15th century, people still had some weird ideas about the Earth, like believing that people in the south lived upside down and had feet on their heads. But everyone knew that the Earth was round – the ancient Greeks had worked that out. So Columbus knew he wouldn't fall off the edge. However, the Greeks also said that the Earth was far smaller that it is – so the East Indies were much further away than Columbus expected.

CAST LIST

- Brave admiral
- Revolting crew
- Americans (lots and lots)

Christopher Columbus (1451–1506)

Columbus was from Italy but was working for Spain when he crossed the Atlantic (it's a long story…). After his first voyage to the Americas he made three more. He hoped to achieve wealth and fame, and felt cheated when he didn't. He also had a reputation as a bit of a dictator, so he wasn't necessarily a great hero. He was obviously a brilliant sailor, though.

Where's the Great Wall?

No one knows where this happened (Columbus wasn't the first to see land, but he took the credit). It was probably an island in the Bahamas. Columbus pressed on to what he expected to be Japan, but then decided was China. In fact, it was Cuba. The next stop he again mistook for Japan – but this time it was the island of Hispaniola (now shared by Haiti and the Dominican Republic). At least Hispaniola had stuff Columbus could take home to prove that he wasn't a complete idiot: gold, parrots, slaves … even a few spices.

Pig-headed

Columbus headed home convinced he had found east Asia. He never changed his mind – despite three more voyages and evidence from other explorers that he was mistaken.

wOOSH!

TO THE STATES

Little HISTORY

c.1003: Vikings are the first Europeans in Americas

1492: Columbus's first voyage

1502: Columbus's last voyage

DESTROY AN EMPIRE ...
WITH 16 HORSES

The Aztec ruled a mighty empire in central Mexico. It was toppled by a band of enemies who would squeeze into a single jumbo jet.

To be more accurate, the 25 million Aztec were overthrown by 508 soldiers, about 100 sailors ... and 16 horses. They were Spaniards (the men, not necessarily the horses) led by Hernán Cortés. They landed on the Mexican coast in February 1519 and made their way towards the Aztec capital, Tenochtitlán.

Cortés was welcomed by the Aztec ruler, Moctezuma II (sometimes called Montezuma), but the Aztec later besieged Cortés's warriors. During the Spaniards' escape, Moctezuma was somehow killed. Cortés gathered his local allies and in 1521 he captured the city and overthrew the empire.

Cortés and the others had sailed from Spain's islands in the Caribbean.

According to the Spaniards, he was wounded when he tried to stop the Aztec attacking them.

WHO WAS WHO?

The Conquistadors

Hernán Cortés was one of a breed of adventurers the Spanish called *conquistadors* ('conquerors'). They used violence to enlarge the Spanish empire and make converts for the Catholic Church. But they also amassed great riches and power: Cortés became governor of Mexico and made a fortune.

HIS HEART'S NOT REALLY IN THIS

Little HISTORY

February 1519: Cortés lands in Mexico

November 1519: Cortés arrives in Tenochtitlán

July 1520: Moctezuma killed; Spaniards flee Tenochtitlán

August 1521: Capture of Tenochtitlán; end of empire

48

CAST LIST

- 25 million Aztec
- A god who turns out not to be a god
- 16 horses

Human sacrifice

Everyone knows that the Aztec killed loads of people for their gods. The victims were stretched out by priests on the top of pyramids while another priest cut out their hearts with a knife. The bodies were thrown down the pyramid steps. But why? The Aztec believed that, if the gods didn't get blood, they might destroy the world. Their warriors captured sacrifices in wars against their neighbours – but without hurting them: the gods didn't want anyone who wasn't perfect. (Sounds like a good idea to have a scar!)

Resentful rebels

Why was the conquest so easy? One reason is that a lot of the 25 million Aztec weren't actually Aztec. They were people the Aztec had (conquered) … and they were kind of mad about losing thousands of citizens as sacrifices to Aztec gods. They joined Cortés to fight their hated rulers.

Doña Marina, a Nahua Mexican, helped Cortés form alliances with other peoples.

Gee up horsey

The Spaniards also had an advantage when it came to actual fighting. The Aztec had never seen horses, which didn't live in the Americas. The beasts frightened them, as well as making the Spanish warriors mobile. Oh, and the Spanish also had cannons. That helped, of course. The Aztec were only armed with spears and bows.

WARNING LONG DROP!

Mythleading myth

According to a story that may or may not be true, Moctezuma believed that Cortés was the Aztec god Quetzalcoatl. Cortés looked just as the god was usually described (an unlucky coincidence for the Aztec). So when a pale-skinned man with a beard arrived by sea from the east, as the myths predicted, Moctezuma welcomed him in. Oh dear.

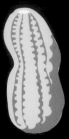

BUY AN ISLAND ...
FOR PEANUTS

With 1.6 million people living on a small island, it's not much wonder that Manhattan is home to some of the most expensive property anywhere in the world.

Things were different in 1524, when an Italian explorer became the first European to see the island, then home to the Lenape people. But it was already clear that Manhattan had a fantastic position. It stood on a natural harbour, protected on the one side by the Hudson River (named for the explorer Henry Hudson, who sailed up it in 1609) and on the other by the East River (named because, er, it's on the east side of the island). The first European settlement in the region was started by Dutch fur traders in 1624. The next year Peter Minuit began building a fort at the bottom of Manhattan Island to protect settlers and guard access to the rivers.

There was a boom in Europe for all sorts of fur, especially beaver, which was used to make hats.

CAST LIST

- **An island**
- **Fur traders**
- **Native Americans**

Little HISTORY

1524: Giovanni da Verrazzano sails into New York Bay

1609: Henry Hudson reports that Manhattan has abundant beavers for fur

1624: Dutch fur traders found New Amsterdam

1625: Peter Minuit builds a fort on southern Manhattan

1626: The Dutch 'buy' Manhattan from the Lenape

1647: Peter Stuyvesant becomes director general

1664: The British conquer the colony; they later rename it New York

I'll GIVE you a few beads for it!!!

A CAPITAL IDEA

In 1788 New York City became the first capital of the United States. It lost the position after a couple of years – as if New Yorkers cared. They might lack political power, but their city was the economic capital of the nation.

Let's make a deal

The Dutch made a deal with the Lenape. They swapped goods worth about 60 guilders for the island. One estimate says that today that would be the equivalent of about $1,000 (which wouldn't buy 1 square metre on Manhattan now). That might not sound like a good deal for the Lenape. Perhaps it wasn't. Native Americans had no real idea of property ownership: they thought the land belonged to everyone. In addition, they did have other territory they could move to. And they did far better than other native groups, who simply had their land taken by European settlers.

In the 19th century the Lakota leader Crazy Horse said 'One does not sell the land people walk on'.

Name change

The colony of New Amsterdam grew up around the Dutch fort, under director general Peter Stuyvesant. In 1664 the settlement was taken over by the English; although the Dutch won it back again, they decided not to keep it. In 1674 a treaty transferred the colony to the English, who gave it a new name: New York.

The original Dutch settlement was at the very tip of the island.

WARNING COSTS A PACKET!

WHO WAS WHO?

Peter Stuyvesant (c.1612–1672)

The last director general of New Amsterdam was a former soldier named Peter Stuyvesant, who arrived in 1647. He built a protective barrier north of the settlement (now the location of Wall Street) and began the avenue that later became Broadway. He also took over the nearby colony of New Sweden. Stuyvesant could be stern and intolerant. He tried to keep Quakers and Jews out of the colony. When the British arrived in 1664, Stuyvesant surrendered, having first made sure that the British would treat the citizens well.

DESTROY A CITY ...
WITH A LOAF OF BREAD

Wooden houses creak, which makes it difficult to sneak downstairs for a midnight feast. Oh, and they also burn. Very easily.

London was the biggest city in 17th-century England. It had about half a million inhabitants. So many people lived in its historic centre that wooden buildings crowded in on twisting streets and narrow alleys. There were open fires everywhere for cooking and heating ... and no fire brigade. When a fire broke out, church bells rang to get volunteers to throw buckets of water on the flames.

CAST LIST

- Useless baker
- Useless mayor
- Wooden houses
- Strong winds

HISS!

Little HISTORY

Sunday 2nd September, 1666: Fire breaks out

Tuesday 4th: St. Paul's Cathedral burns down

Wednesday 5th: Fire burns out

That baker's a pudding!

And fires did break out – lots of fires. But the fire that broke out after midnight on Sunday 2nd September, 1666, was the worst of all. It started in a bakery in Pudding Lane, near the north end of London Bridge. The baker's family escaped (their maid was not so lucky), but sparks set light to nearby homes. As the fire pulled air into burning buildings, strong winds spread more sparks. By dawn a stretch of buildings was on fire.

In those days, London Bridge had houses on it.

WARNING BURNT CRUST!

Call the fire brigade …

The fire burned for three days and destroyed much of the old city – including St. Paul's Cathedral. Homeless Londoners camped outside the city walls. Some blamed the mayor for not stopping the fire sooner; others said that it had been started by the French, who were about to invade England. By the end of the fire, over 13,000 homes had been destroyed, most of them belonging to poor workers. Only a handful of people are reported to have died – but as no one really recorded the facts, we may never know the true number.

The mayor had actually said the fire was so small that someone could wee it out – OOPS!

SIZZLE!

When the past was RUBBISH

You woodn't like it (geddit?!)

In the 17th century most cities had fires all the time. The problem was wood. Virtually all houses were built of planks that burned easily. The streets were so narrow that fire jumped easily from building to building. There were potential sources of fire everywhere: stoves, fireplaces, candles, lamps, even cigars. And nowhere had fire brigades. In most cities volunteers formed long lines to pass buckets of water from a river or pump to throw onto the flames. If they had time, they pulled down buildings around the fire to create a gap that the flames couldn't jump across.

MODERNIZE A COUNTRY ...
BY HAVING A SHAVE

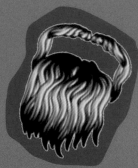

You've probably had your parents telling you when you need a hair cut. But imagine if it was the emperor telling you ...

OK, Peter the Great wasn't mainly worried about hair. When he became sole tsar of Russia in 1696 he had great ambitions. But he believed that Russia's future lay with Europe to the west, not with Asia. In Europe, the so-called Age of Reason was producing lots of new ideas. Peter set out in disguise to see what was happening. (His disguise didn't work very well, as he took loads of other Russians with him.) Peter came home with new ideas about all sorts of things – ships, dentistry, lepidopterology (er, butterflies and moths), fire hoses. And he was convinced that he needed to modernize Russia.

He really became tsar in 1682 but he was only 10, so had to share power with his mum and brother.

Little HISTORY

1682: Peter becomes joint tsar

1696: Becomes sole tsar

1697: Travels to western Europe

1698: Returns to Russia

1703: Founds St. Petersburg

Modernize your DAD

WHAT YOU'LL NEED
An old-fashioned dad (in other words, any ordinary dad)

1 Make a list of the most old-fashioned things about your dad.
2 Come up with a modern equivalent for each item on the list. If your dad is bald, say, try spraying his head with metallic paint. Swap his cardigan for a hoodie.
3 Send him outside so people can admire his new look (but don't let him look in a mirror first).

WHO WAS WHO?

Peter the Great (1672–1725)

Peter achieved his ambition of reforming Russia. His wars against the Ottoman Empire and Sweden helped make Russia a major military and naval power. Meanwhile, he severely limited the power of Russia's nobles, the Boyars (that was who Peter's beard tax was mainly aimed at). That left the tsar with far more control over the country.

A close shave

First, Russia needed a new capital. Peter hired architects to build St. Petersburg on the coast of the Baltic Sea. Second, he went to war to gain more ports, so Russia could become a naval power. And third, he made everyone shave off their beards. Medieval Russians were pretty hairy (the men, at least). It was traditional to have beards – but Peter had noticed that other Europeans did not. He decided that beards were old fashioned, so in 1698 he ordered his officials and soldiers to cut off their beards. A few years later, he put a tax on beards. Men who paid it received a silver token stamped with the words 'the beard is a superfluous burden'. Out went traditional Russian clothes, too. Peter wanted his court officials to dress like Europeans as a sign that they were looking forward to a modern future.

SNIP! SNIP!

CAST LIST

- Peter the Great
- Hairy Russians
- Barbers

GET RID OF A RUBBISH KING
WITH AN AXE

Being a ruler is cool... You get to wear a crown and boss everyone around. But if a king or queen goes too far – watch out! If their subjects get angry enough, they might take drastic action.

The English were the first, when they got rid of King Charles I in 1649. They gave the king the chop (literally) and got Parliament to run the country. The experiment might have worked, but Parliament turned out to be a miserable bunch. So after 11 years the English got themselves a new monarch – Charles II, son of the dead king – and they've never tried without one since.

CAST LIST

- Axe
- Axeman
- Angry subjects
- Bad king

Sacre bleu!

In the 18th century, the idea of a monarch became even stronger. A theory known as absolutism suggested that monarchs had a 'divine right' to rule however they wanted – as long as they looked after their subjects. But the French writer Jean-Jacques Rousseau argued that, under what he called the 'social contract', the monarch can only rule with the agreement of his or her subjects.

I wasn't that bad!

Little HISTORY

1642: Civil war in England, royalists vs Parliament

1649: Victory for Parliament, Charles I executed

1660: The Restoration, Charles II becomes king

1789: French Revolution

1792: Execution of King Louis XVI

1814: Constitutional monarchy restored in France

CHOP- CHOP!

HE AIN'T HEAVY, HE'S THE KING!

In 1649 the English Parliament announced: 'The office of the king in this nation is unnecessary, burdensome and dangerous to the liberty, society and public interest of the people.' Of course, when Parliament asked Charles II to become king in 1660, everyone forgot that the monarchy was so useless!

The two theories clashed in France at the end of the 18th century. Many people objected to how the Bourbon dynasty and the court dominated the country while everyone else paid for them in the form of taxes. When the king and the parlement failed to resolve their problems, the French revolted in 1789. They replaced the monarchy with a republic. The revolutionaries executed so many members of the ruling class, or Ancien Régime, they used the new super-fast guillotine to take off their heads. The blade came down on King Louis XVI in 1792. Once that happened, monarchs everywhere in Europe soon got the message: use your powers responsibly ... or else!

The guillotine was invented in 1791 by J. I. Guillotin, as a less painful way to execute criminals. He should know – he was a doctor!

WARNING HURTS A BIT!

SETTLE A NEW CONTINENT ...
BY GETTING RID OF CONVICTS

In the late 18th century Britain had a crime problem. Because the poor were so poor that they kept stealing to survive; there were too many convicts to fit in the prisons.

Of course, the authorities could have come up with lighter punishments for minor crimes. Instead they tried sending prisoners (abroad) – for life. The British had sent criminals to their colonies in North America, but U.S. independence halted that. Luckily, in 1770 Captain James Cook claimed a (new land) in the Pacific that he said was ideal for settlement. In May 1787, ships set off for Botany Bay with 775 convicts and another 645 officials and crew. It took eight months to reach Botany Bay ... and about eight minutes to realize that Cook was wrong. The soil was too sandy to grow crops. The fleet moved along the coast to Sydney Cove.

Sending criminals abroad was called transportation.

Cook came ashore at Botany Bay, Australia, near the modern city of Sydney.

CAST LIST

- James Cook
- 162,000 convicts (not all at once)

When the past was RUBBISH

Hanged for a sheep

Transportation was one of only two major punishments for criminals in late 18th-century Britain... The other was hanging. The law protected property, no matter what. Even poaching a rabbit could lead to being sent to Australia (even if the culprit was pardoned by the court).

Port Arthur nightmare!

Port Arthur on Tasmania was known as 'Hell on Earth'. Inmates broke rocks and mined coal; they slept in tiny, dark cells. Escape was virtually impossible: the prison was cut off by shark-infested seas.

Port Arthur

Can you milk a cow?

The new site was little better. People began to starve. There weren't any farmers among the convicts to grow food – and not enough livestock. A second fleet arrived in 1790, but it just brought more starving convicts. Anyone who tried to escape from Botany Bay usually died in the Outback.

WARNING
NO
ESCAPE!

Settling down

By the end of 1790, things were better. Supplies arrived from South Africa. A convict started a farm. New prison colonies were set up. For another 80 years, convicts were transported to help build the colonies. When they were freed, many stayed on. New settlers arrived. Australia became a place where people wanted to live. It was on its way.

Little HISTORY

1788: First Fleet arrives
1790: Second Fleet arrives
1817: The continent is named 'Australia'
1868: Last convicts reach Western Australia

G'DAY!

LOSE AN EMPIRE...
OVER A CUP OF TEA

Britain governed colonies in North America for centuries before Americans began to think that they should govern themselves.

Little HISTORY

1765: Stamp Act
1768: Boycott of British goods
1770: Boston Massacre
1773: Boston Tea Party
1774: Intolerable Acts
1775: American Revolution

Colonial Americans were governed from London, with governors appointed by the British king. They were also subject to British taxes – but there were no American members of Parliament to (speak up) when it came to deciding how those taxes were spent.

Americans called for 'No taxation without representation'.

Talking taxes

The situation came to a head when the British imposed new taxes in the 1760s. Some British politicians warned King George III about over-taxing the colonies, but he needed as much money as he could get. His government had to pay for its wars against France for control of Canada. The British thought the Americans should pay. First they taxed trade with the West Indies, another British colony, even though it was just next door in the Caribbean. Then they imposed a Stamp Tax on all legal documents (and playing cards!).

CAST LIST

- Mad king
- Colonials
- Tea (milk and two sugars, please)

Shall I pour?

Another new tax was placed on tea – which the Americans loved – even though taxes on tea were being cut in Britain at the same time. In October 1773 ships carrying tea docked in Boston Harbor (tea could only be carried on British ships).

Bostonians were already angry with the British after British soldiers had shot dead colonial protestors in the 'Boston Massacre' of 1770. Now the governor refused to pay the tax on the tea or to let the ships leave. On 16 December, 1773, some 200 colonials went on board and dumped the tea overboard into the harbour. Some people were dressed as native Mohawks, but no-one was fooled.

Belligerent Boston

In reply to the 'Boston Tea Party' the British closed Boston port and put Massachusetts Colony – to which Boston belonged – under royal government. The Americans called these the 'Intolerable Acts'. When British soldiers began to search for weapons stored by Americans, the colonials fought back – the American Revolution had begun. By the time it was over Britain would have lost its North American colonies and the United States would be born.

When the past was RUBBISH

Consternated colonials

The colonies in North America had originally relied on Britain for imports, military defence – and more settlers. As time passed, however, the colonies became more self-sufficient. Their cities grew wealthy. Their possessions were made in America. Their population was growing. So people wondered why Britain still got to govern the colonies. It seemed to men like Bostonian Sam Adams that this made no sense. They began to dream of governing themselves.

ANOTHER CUPPA?

TEA

TEA

TEA

WARNING NO SALT WATER!

TEA

INDUSTRY & EMPIRE

About 250 years ago, the world started changing more quickly. One reason was the coming of industry; another was contact between cultures on opposite sides of the Earth. Despite all the changes, people still made history with odd ideas.

1865

1859

Beaks speak

CREATE A LAND OF THE FREE ...
WITH SLAVE LABOUR

The Liberty Bell rang out after the Declaration of Independence created the United States of America in 1776 – but it turned out that not everyone got to be free.

The Declaration of Independence was full of good ideas – the United States is still based on them nearly 250 years later. It included a line that everyone knows: 'All men are created equal'. That meant that the king couldn't push the Americans around. (George III had irritated them by charging high taxes without asking them how the money should be spent). The British, at whom the Declaration was aimed, pointed out that its claims of equality were all very well – but what about the 500,000 slaves in America? All men might be equal, but it seemed that some were less equal than others.

Most of the Declaration was a list of things the king had done wrong.

Little HISTORY

1619: First slaves in North America
1776: Declaration of Independence
1863: Emancipation of the slaves

When the past was RUBBISH

The Middle Passage

The 'Middle Passage' was the slaves' journey from Africa to America. Having been imprisoned in forts on the African coast they were chained up below decks on cramped ships for voyages that could last months. They were fed poorly and many fell sick. When they were allowed on deck for exercise, many committed suicide by jumping overboard. Up to 15 percent of slaves died on the voyage.

Sally Hemings (c.1773–1835)

Sally Hemings was a mixed-race slave owned by Thomas Jefferson, writer of the Declaration of Independence and third president of the United States. Because her family was light skinned, they were high in the slave hierarchy at Jefferson's estate, Monticello. As a teenager, Sally spent two years in Paris, where Jefferson served as ambassador. There were rumours that Sally gave birth to Jefferson's son after the death of his wife.

Slave state

Of the 56 men who signed the Declaration, about a third owned slaves. Its main author, Thomas Jefferson, had about 150 slaves. George Washington, the country's first president, owned more than 300. So what was all that stuff about men being created equal?

When the Founders wrote a Constitution, they counted a slave as being equal to three-fifths of a white citizen.

In black and white

The simple fact was that most white Americans saw black Americans as an inferior race, even if they weren't slaves. They thought government was best organized by educated, white males (which might be why the Declaration didn't say anything about all women or Native Americans being created equal, either).

CAST LIST
- White male Americans
- All other Americans

We the People

insure domestic Tranquility, provide for the common defence and our Posterity, do ordain and establish this Constitution

START AN INDUSTRIAL REVOLUTION ...
WITH A KETTLE

Steam trains, steamships, modern coal mining and iron working, factories, textile mills, farm machinery – the whole lot started with a cup of tea.

In fact, they all started with the steam engine – and the steam engine started with a cup of tea. The first really useful one, anyway. Steam engines were already 50 years old when Scottish engineer James Watt was asked to repair an early version called a Newcomen engine in 1764.

Warning! Science bit ahead ...

It's useful to know a bit about steam engines, so here is a detailed explanation... Water goes in cylinder. Boils. Makes steam. Steam expands. Pushes piston. Steam cools. Becomes water. Piston falls back. More steam. Piston pushed. Steam turns to water. Piston falls. And so on. And on. OK? Any questions?

CAST LIST

● Brainy Scot (there were a lot of them about!)

Early steam engines were often used to pump water out of coal and tin mines.

Gas (steam) fills more space than liquid (water), which is how it pushes the piston.

CHOO! CHOO!

66

WHISTLE!

Hoots mon!
Watt was one of many
brainy Scots inventors:
- William Murdoch
  – gas lights
- Charles MacIntosh
  – raincoat
- James Young Simpson
  – chloroform
- Kirkpatrick MacMillan
  – bicycle

Fancy a cuppa?

According to legend, Watt was watching a kettle boil when he had a revelation. He saw that alternately heating and cooling a cylinder to produce and condense steam wasted energy. He invented an engine that let the steam escape into a condenser, so the cylinder stayed hot all the time. Suddenly the steam engine was three times more efficient.

Driving force

Watt built his first engine in 1776. He also invented gears and cranks to turn the engine's up-and-down motion into rotary motion. That made it useful for driving lathes, looms – just about anything!

Little HISTORY

1712: Newcomen engine
1776: Watt engine
1829: Stephenson's *Rocket*

WHO WAS WHO?

James Watt (1736–1819)

Watt and his business partner, Matthew Boulton, built more than 500 Watt engines. Watt also came up with other innovations, such as using horsepower to measure power. Today the standard unit for power is the Watt – named in his honour.

CONQUER AFRICA ...
WITH A PIECE OF WOOD

For 19th-century Europeans Africa was full of mystery. They knew little about it. Explorers tended not to come back.

The 'dark continent' was said to be home to great and wealthy empires. Vast (caravans) carried gold out from its heart across the Sahara Desert. Europeans wanted to grab some of Africa's riches for themselves. It made it easier, of course, that most Europeans did not think Africans had any right to their own wealth. They saw black Africans as being inferior to whites.

Caravans with camels – not like you see on the motorway.

BUZZ!

Let's stick to the beach

European knowledge of Africa was limited to the north and to the coasts. Africa was known as 'the white man's graveyard'. Many would-be explorers and settlers died of disease – and the biggest killer of all was malaria.

WHERE AM I?

WHO WAS WHO?

David Livingstone (1813–1873)

Scottish missionary David Livingstone was the most famous explorer of Africa. He travelled widely in southern and central Africa. When he was not heard of for some years, Henry Stanley successfully found him near Lake Tanganyika in 1871. Livingstone died in Africa: his heart was buried there.

Little HISTORY

1820: Quinine produced
1841: Livingstone in Africa
1885: Europeans divide Africa
1914: Europeans rule Africa

Monster mozzies

Malaria was carried on a parasite that lived on the mosquito, and was transmitted by mosquito bite. Europeans had no resistance to it (most Africans did). There was a cure ... but it came from the other side of the world.

Tree-mendous

Spanish explorers in South America had noticed that people used extracts from cinchona bark to cure malaria. But it was only in 1820 that French scientists made a modern anti-malarial drug from it: quinine.

Quinine allowed explorers to go to places which malaria had made too dangerous. The world was open to exploration – and exploitation. The 'scramble for Africa' was on. By 1914, most of the continent was under European rule.

The tree was named after a Peruvian countess who was cured in 1630.

Explorers' club

Among the Europeans who opened Africa in the 19th century were:
- Mungo Park
  – River Niger, 1805
- Henry Morton Stanley
  – Congo, 1880s
- Burton and Speke
  – Great Lakes, 1860s
- Heinrich Barth
  – Sudan, 1850s

WARNING
BLOOD SUCKER!

DR LIVINGSTONE I PRESUME?

ER, NO, ACTUALLY!

CAST LIST

- Explorers
- Mosquitos
- A South American tree

DEFEAT A KILLER DISEASE ...
WITH A MAP

Victorian London was an exciting place – and it was rich. But there was one problem ... well, tens of thousands of problems: Londoners.

Many people had no jobs or money. They lived in crowded slums known as 'rookeries'. Dozens of families got their water from communal pumps and got rid of their waste in open drains and cesspits (yuck). Conditions were so bad that disease often broke out.

Let's clear the air

In 1854 a cholera epidemic killed over 500 people near Broad Street, in the Soho district. Doctors blamed a miasma of 'bad air' – except one. Yorkshire physician John Snow was working in London. He didn't believe that cholera was spread through the air (though of course he didn't actually know how it was spread, because no one had yet discovered the existence of germs).

Miasma - Greek for 'pollution' - was blamed for disease from ancient times until germs were discovered in 1861.

When the past was RUBBISH

The Great Stink

In 1858 an emergency nearly forced the British Parliament out of London. The River Thames just outside the windows smelled so bad that MPs could barely breathe. They kept the curtains closed and soaked them in lime to try to stop the stench. The whole city stank. The river overflowed with sewage from cesspits, along with filth from businesses such as slaughterhouses. A hot summer made the water smell like an open lavatory (which it was, essentially). It was only after the Great Stink that London's modern sewers were built.

- Germs
(unknown then)
- Doctor with a map
- 500 dead

Pump action

Snow talked to residents of Soho (though lots of people had fled the area). He transferred what he learned to a map, shading houses where people had died. Guess what? Most were clustered around a water pump in Broad Street. Snow guessed that the pump was the source of the infection. He didn't know the precise reason, but he guessed correctly that it had to do with drinking water and sewage being too close together. Snow got the council to remove the handle from the pump – and the cholera outbreak dwindled away.

KNOCK-OUT DOC!

Working out that cholera was transmitted by infected water was not John Snow's only contribution to medicine. He also pioneered using chloroform and ether as anaesthetics. The gas knocked patients out during surgery. Snow even anaesthetised Queen Victoria during the births of two of her children. In 2003 British doctors voted him the greatest ever British doctor.

WARNING
NASTY
GERMS!

Little
HISTORY

1849: John Snow studies causes of cholera
1854: Snow maps Broad Street outbreak
1861: Germ theory of disease

TURN SCIENCE ON ITS HEAD ...
WITH A CHAFFINCH

Charles Darwin wasn't the first man to say that all animals had evolved from earlier animals, but he was the first to say how. A little birdie told him...

As a young man, Darwin shared his family's interest in natural history. In 1831 Charles got a chance to make a five-year voyage around the world on HMS *Beagle* (he was hired to keep the captain company). The trip would change Darwin's life ... and the history of science.

Everywhere the ship stopped, Darwin studied plants and animals. On the Galapagos Islands, which lay in the Pacific Ocean 975 kilometres off the coast of Ecuador, Darwin found unique species such as the iguana (a giant lizard) and a whole range of finches that lived on different islands. The island species had evolved in isolation, so they were especially interesting to Darwin.

CAST LIST
- Charles Darwin
- Finches
- Humans (who are really apes)

WHO WAS WHO?

Charles Darwin (1809–1882)

Charles Darwin set out to be a doctor, but he gave up his studies to concentrate on marine invertebrates (shellfish, to you and me). When he sailed on HMS *Beagle*, it was his reports on geology that made him famous. *On the Origin of Species* and another book, *The Descent of Man*, cemented Darwin's reputation as the man who discovered evolution – although, in fact, other writers had done a lot of work, too.

WHO'S A PRETTY BOY THEN?

FASCINATING FINCHES

In the Galapagos, Darwin noticed that the finches on different islands had differently shaped beaks. Some were short and stubby while others were long and thin; a third type was hooked.

Darwin concluded that all the finches were descended from common ancestors – maybe finches that were blown to the islands by the wind. But the finches on each island had evolved beaks suited to the best food on their island, such as nectar from flowers, or nuts or seeds.

If birds on an island could get more food if they had longer beaks, over time more birds with longer beaks would reproduce than birds with shorter beaks. Eventually all the birds on the island would have long beaks. Hey presto! Natural selection!

I said fittest, not fattest ...

Darwin's studies led to his theory of evolution: that animals evolve to gain themselves an advantage, such as being able to get more food or find a mate more easily. Darwin called this natural selection, or 'the survival of the fittest'.

In 1859 Darwin wrote up his theory in a book called *On the Origin of Species by Means of Natural Selection*. The book caused a sensation. Not only did it contradict the idea that God created humans in his own image; it also suggested that humans were descended from apes. Most people could see that Darwin's theory made a lot of sense – but it was still controversial. So controversial, in fact, that some people still reject it (but most scientists accept that it is true).

Little HISTORY

1831: Sails on the *Beagle*
1859: Writes *On the Origin of Species*
1871: Writes *The Descent of Man*

ABOLISH SLAVERY ...
WITH A STORY BOOK

The campaign against slavery led the United States to civil war. President Abraham Lincoln was only half joking when he blamed the war on a book by a young author.

CAST LIST

- **4 million slaves**
- **Female boffin**
- **Good president**
- **Uncle Tom**

Harriet Beecher Stowe was no ordinary woman. Her father, Lyman Beecher, was a famous preacher. He made sure Harriet had a good (education;) she became a preacher, like her father, and a bit of a boffin (she married another, Professor Calvin Ellis Stowe). The Stowes were abolitionists, or supporters of the campaign to abolish slavery. They even sheltered slaves who were escaping along a secret route to freedom in the North.

At the time, most girls did not study academic subjects.

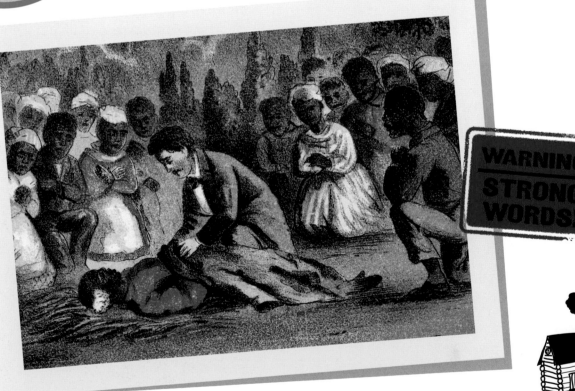

The men who beat Tom to death in Uncle Tom's Cabin are converted to Christianity by witnessing his faith as he dies.

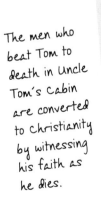

WARNING
STRONG
WORDS!

I REALLY SHOULD READ THAT BOOK

EMANCIPATION

Little HISTORY

1850: Fugitive Slave Act

1852: *Uncle Tom's Cabin* published

1853: *Uncle Tom's Cabin* sells 300,000 copies in its first year

1854: Supporters of slavery and abolitionists fight in Kansas

1860: Abraham Lincoln is elected US president; Southern states leave the Union

1861: The Civil War begins

1863: The Emancipation Proclamation frees all slaves in rebel states

1865: Defeat of the South; Lincoln is assassinated

Abraham Lincoln (1809–1865)

One of the most revered of all Americans, Lincoln was an Illinois lawyer famous for his honesty. He sparked a crisis when he became president in 1860 because he opposed slavery. Southern states left the Union – and Lincoln went to war to protect it. In 1863 he issued the Emancipation Proclamation, so the war became a fight to free the slaves.

Arguing Americans

The debate about slavery was bitter. The Southern economy depended on slaves, but in the North slavery was illegal. Many Northerners thought it was immoral to own human beings as property. Then, in 1850, Congress passed the Fugitive Slave Act. It forced people to return escaped slaves to their owners – even from states where slavery was illegal. Northerners were outraged.

Powerful book

Harriet Beecher Stowe decided to write about slave life. Her novel, *Uncle Tom's Cabin*, told of the Christian slave Uncle Tom, his suffering, his faith and his martyrdom – when the dying slave forgives the men who beat him to death. Harriet's description of slave life was a powerful argument for abolition. When she met Abraham Lincoln during the Civil War, the president commented 'So you are the little woman who wrote the book that started this great war!'

'Uncle Tom's Cabin' was the second-bestselling book of the 19th century – after the Bible!

SHARE OUT A DESERT ...
WITH A RULER

Take a look at a map of North Africa. There are a lot of straight borders – but they're not following any natural features.

North Africa has many different peoples with their own cultures and languages. For centuries they inhabited the Sahara Desert, the mountains and scrublands and the Mediterranean coast. They didn't really have countries or borders. Some were nomads, anyway, and never stayed in one place. That system worked for thousands of years. But when Europeans built up empires in Africa in the 19th century, they soon decided it didn't suit them.

Early kingdoms had strong centres, but ran into each other at their edges.

CAST LIST
- European officials
- 'Empty' deserts (ignore the people who lived there!)

1

12 13

Scrambled up

European countries were racing to set up colonies that would provide resources and a market for the goods they produced. In the 1880s and 1890s they began the 'Scramble for Africa'. Everyone got involved, even tiny Belgium.

In 1884 the European powers met in Berlin to share out Africa (they didn't bother to ask the Africans). Where there were no obvious borders, like mountains or rivers, they simply drew a line on the map. They didn't really care: desert land wasn't very useful. But their lines divided clans' territory or nomads' routes in a random way. When countries formed later, they kept the borders – but in the middle of the desert, it still didn't make much difference to the people living there. There aren't many fences or customs officers!

Greedy king

The Congo Free State in central Africa wasn't like other colonies. The Belgian king, Leopold II, owned it as his private property. His men forced Africans to collect rubber. If the Africans failed to meet their targets, the Belgians often cut off their hands.

Share out your HOUSE

TRY THIS

WHAT YOU'LL NEED
graph paper
pencil
ruler
ball of string
boxing gloves

1 On the paper, carefully draw a scale map of your house.
2 With the ruler, divide the map into the same number of sections as there are family members.
3 Use the string to mark out the dividing lines in each room.
4 Tell each member of the family which area he or she has to stick to (this may be when you need the boxing gloves).

Little HISTORY

1879: Britain and France take control of Egypt
1881: France occupies Tunisia
1882: Britain takes over the Ottoman empire, including Sudan
1884: Berlin Conference

The EAGLE has landed...

1969

THE MODERN WORLD

The modern world stretches from nearly a hundred years ago until right now. You'll recognize nearly everything about it ... but there might be a few things that come as a bit more of a surprise.

1947

Dribble, dribble, drip, drip

FIGHT A WAR ...
BY SITTING STILL

For most of World War I, the Western Front barely moved. Advancing a few metres could cost thousands – or hundreds of thousands – of lives.

In August 1914, Germany was threatened by Russia ... so it invaded France. What?! The Germans did not want to fight on two fronts, so they planned to defeat France quickly before fighting Russia. The plan nearly worked. They got within 50 kilometres of Paris, but the French and British pushed them back.

Both sides dug in, which consisted of, er, digging. Lots of digging. Troops dug lines of trenches that were separated by only a few hundred metres of no-man's-land, which was guarded by miles of barbed wire. Miles and miles of trench networks grew up. Artillery shells killed the grass and trees and churned up the ground into mud.

The Germans were so close to Paris that the French sent reinforcements to the battle by taxi.

Little HISTORY

1914: War begins; trenches dug
1915: Trenches stuck in place
1916: Trenches stuck in place
1917: Allied breakout
1918: War ends

CAST LIST

- 1 million Germans
- 1 million French
- 1 million British
- Some Belgians

KA-
BOOM!

Let's try that again

On both sides, commanders tried different tactics to get through the trench defences. They usually involved shelling of enemy lines followed by an infantry attack. At the sound of a whistle, men climbed from the trenches and went 'over the top'. Often they advanced into machine-gun fire. Both sides made small gains at different times but usually lost them in an enemy counterattack. The Western Front barely moved. One soldier said that it was like a sausage grinder that was screwed in place – and kept turning out mangled flesh.

Breakout!

It would not be until 1917 that the Allies managed to break the deadlock. A final push got through the line. The Germans began to retreat. Eventually they had no choice but to surrender.

Outbreak of War

When an Austrian archduke was murdered by Serbs in 1914, a system of alliances began to operate. The Russians supported the Serbs, the Germans the Austrians. Germany planned to defeat France before fighting Russia, so it invaded Belgium, which was protected by Britain. In just a few days, much of Europe was at war.

WIN THE VOTE ...
WITH AN IRON CHAIN

In a democracy, all adults get to vote, right? Wrong! For centuries, only the rich had the right to vote – and they didn't want to share it ... especially not with women.

That was true even in ancient Athens, the home of democracy. Everyone was entitled to vote ... as long as they were male citizens. That ruled out women, foreigners and slaves: nearly nine-tenths of the population.

The word comes from the Greek words demos and kratos, 'people' and 'power'.

Men get mean

Thousands of years later, at the start of the 20th century, not much had changed. Many men still believed that women shouldn't be involved in politics. Some argued that women weren't educated enough to understand current affairs (of course, they could have tried educating women better). Not surprisingly, women objected.

By 1900 some women could vote – but only in New Zealand!

CAST LIST
- Chains
- Railings
- Impatient women
- Stubborn men

When the past was RUBBISH

Who gets to vote?

Democracy came to Europe slowly from around the 13th century. But usually only landowners were allowed to vote. That meant nobles ... and it meant men (who often voted for their noble friends). But in the 19th century things had to change. The growth of industry created a growing middle class. Factory owners, lawyers and merchants wanted the same rights as landowners. So, governments began to extend the suffrage, or right to vote: to people with a bit less land, then with virtually no land, then with just a house – and finally to all citizens. But still not to women (or slaves, either, in the United States).

Dying to vote

The press named them suffragettes or suffragists.

Some women – and men – were impatient with not having the right to vote. They began to use direct action to make their case. They staged noisy demonstrations. They chained themselves to railings in public places. When they were arrested, they went on hunger strike. The suffragette Emily Davison died when she jumped in front of the King's horse in the 1913 Derby. For some people such acts only proved that women were too emotional to be involved in politics.

She probably did not mean to be killed, as she had bought a return railway ticket to the races.

'X' marks the spot

Then, when World War I broke out in 1914, women took on new roles, including doing 'men's' jobs. More than anything, that persuaded men that women deserved a say in public life. In 1918, the British Parliament gave some women the right to vote; all women got the vote in 1928. In the United States, the Nineteenth Amendment gave women the vote in 1920.

WARNING ANGRY WOMEN!

DAILY VOTER

SUFFRAGETTE ARRESTED

British suffragette Emmeline Pankhurst was arrested after chaining herself to railings outside the Houses of Parliament. Her Women's Social and Political Union was the British suffragette organisation; in the USA it was Alice Paul and Lucy Burns' National Women's Party.

WE WILL NOT BE MOVED!

GET OUT OF A DEPRESSION ...
BY PLANTING TREES

When Franklin D. Roosevelt (FDR) became president in 1932, some 13 million Americans were out of work – up from just 5 million two years earlier. The richest nation on earth had lines of beggars on its streets.

Around the world trade had slowed right down. The Great Depression had begun. It would last most of the decade. In the United States factories were closing and (banks) were failing. Economists believed that the problem was that people who were worried about their jobs didn't spend much, so they didn't buy much. Factories stopped making anything because the warehouses were already full of stuff that wasn't selling. More workers lost their jobs ... and so on.

One of FDR's first actions was to close the banks for a short 'holiday'.

New Deal

FDR wanted to get people to work doing something ... anything. His experts – known as the Brain Trust – came up with a 'New Deal'. Among other plans, the government would employ the jobless, so they would start buying things again and kick-start the economy ... and do some useful work.

CAST LIST

- FDR
- Brain Trust
- 500,000 unemployed
- 3 billion trees

Little HISTORY

1929: Great Depression begins
1932: FDR elected president
1933: CCC created
1936 : FDR reelected
1940 : FDR reelected
1942: CCC disbanded

TIMBER!!

WARNING GREEN SHOOTS!

Franklin D. Roosevelt (1882–1945)

FDR came from an old and privileged family. Despite being crippled by a childhood illness, FDR rose through the Democratic Party before being elected as governor of New York in 1929 and as president in 1932. He was elected another three times – the only president to serve four terms – and guided the United States through both the Great Depression and World War II.

All sorts of new agencies oversaw this work. One of the most successful was the Civilian Conservation Corps or CCC. It recruited 500,000 young men to plant 3 billion trees in wilderness areas. The trees helped prevent erosion (their roots held the soil in place) and would produce valuable wood.

Objections

Not everyone agreed with FDR. They said the government shouldn't be helping people out who ought to learn to stand on their own two feet. For one thing, it was very expensive. For another, it made the government much bigger and gave it more of a role in Americans' lives. That made some people very nervous … and it still does.

When the past was RUBBISH

Hoovervilles

The person who got most blame for the Great Depression was FDR's predecessor as president, Herbert Hoover – mainly because he didn't seem to do much to prevent the crisis. His opponents used the word 'Hooverville' to describe the communities that sprang up near city dumps and railway lines. The jobless and homeless built huts and shacks made of corrugated iron and tar paper. They slept beneath 'Hoover blankets' – old newspapers. When the soles of their shoes wore through, they mended them with 'Hoover leather' – cardboard. If they couldn't afford petrol, they travelled in a 'Hoover wagon' – a car pulled by horses.

INVENT MODERN ART ...
BY SPILLING SOME PAINT

For centuries, paintings looked like things. But around 1870 artists started experimenting with abstracts – and things got out of hand ... and very messy.

S.P.L.A.T!

When photography became popular in the 19th century, some painters began experimenting with new methods. In the 1870s the Impressionists in France tried to capture light effects. In the 1910s the cubists painted real objects – but from different angles. At the same time the Russian Kasimir Malevich began producing abstracts. These paintings weren't 'of' anything.

Cubism was named because it used geometric shapes to show 'facets' of objects.

In the United States

In 1913 the Armory Show in New York brought modern art to America. U.S. artists had often been uncomfortable about the idea of painting in old

LITTLE HISTORY

1874: First Impressionist exhibition, France
1906: Cubism begins
1913: Armory Show
1915: Malevich paints *Black Square*
1947: Pollock's "drip paintings"

TRY THIS

Paint your own MODERN ART

WHAT YOU'LL NEED

plastic sheet
A3 paper
liquid house paint or poster paint (different colors)
tolerant parents
carpet cleaner*
(*in case of emergencies)

1 Put down the plastic sheet to protect the floor.
2 Lie the paper on top of it.
3 Use the paint to dribble and drip patterns on the paper.
4 Check the floor for spills.
5 Clear up any mess.
6 Ring the Museum of Modern Art.

DriBBle

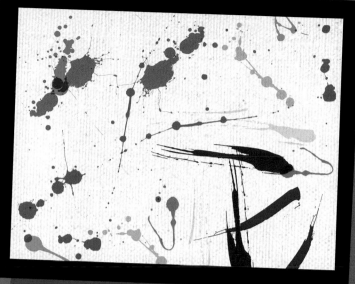

BORING

EXCITING!

European styles. Many loved the idea of exploring new ways of painting, which they tried over the following decades.

Styles came and went, but one of the most significant came in the mid–1940s. The artist Jackson Pollock began to make paintings by dripping liquid paint onto huge canvases stretched out on the floor. The way he moved about on top of his work, spilling paint or using a stick to make patterns, gave it the name 'action painting'. Pollock said that the technique allowed him to concentrate on expressing his emotions directly. His critics said that the (drip paintings) looked like they'd been made by children.

TOOL KIT

- Paint
- Canvas
- Mad artist

WHO WAS WHO?

Jackson Pollock (1912–1956)

When *Life* magazine asked in 1949, 'Is he the greatest living painter in the United States?' Jackson Pollock was world famous for his drip paintings. He based them on Navajo sand painting and Mexican murals. He said that he started with an idea of what he wanted the painting to look like and then liked to work 'inside' it. Pollock gave up drip painting in 1950 and tried other styles, but none were so successful. He died in a car crash after driving while drunk.

One of Pollock's drip paintings is one of the most expensive painting in the world – it sold for $140 million at auction!

GO TO THE MOON ...
WITH A
POCKET CALCULATOR

Visiting the moon was an awesome feat – especially because the spacecraft used were less technologically advanced than most modern cars.

If you've got a pocket calculator, then you own a computer far more powerful than anything used on the whole moon mission. NASA scientists had computers to do calculations, but they also did a lot of work in the old fashioned way – with a pencil, paper and loads of sums. The challenge was to fire a rocket across about 38,000 kilometres of space to land on a moving target. No one even knew if it could be done. They did know, however, that it would be risky. The astronauts would be strapped to a rocket that was like a huge missile filled with highly explosive fuel.

NASA stands for the U.S. National Aeronautical and Space Administration

1969

Little HISTORY

1957: First satellite in orbit
1961: Yuri Gagarin, first man in space
1961: JFK begins the U.S. moon programme
1962: Gemini programme
1967: Apollo programme
1969: Moon landing, Apollo 11

WARNING MAY BE CHEESE!

Applaud Apollo

In the summer of 1969 a Saturn V rocket took off carrying Apollo 11. About 110 kilometres above the moon, the lunar module (LM) separated from the command module and began its descent. As the LM approached the landing site, however, the onboard computer could not cope with all the information it was receiving. Astronauts Neil Armstrong and Buzz Aldrin had to take manual control. On 20 July, 1969, humans landed on the moon for the first time.

teflon, used for nonstick pans!

After all that, they only stayed 21 hours and 31 minutes!

TO BOLDLY GO...

WHO WAS WHO?

Neil Armstrong (born 1930)

The first human on the moon was a former Navy pilot who became a test pilot at Edwards Air Force Base in California, pioneering super-fast jet aircraft. Armstrong joined NASA and went into space on Gemini 8 before becoming commander of Apollo 11. As he stepped on to the moon, Armstrong said the famous words: 'That's one small step for a man, one giant leap for mankind.'

BECOME PRESIDENT ...
BY BEING AN ACTOR

Most U.S. presidents have been men like lawyers and generals. In 1980 the 40th president broke the pattern... Ronald Reagan was a famous actor.

Well, kind of famous. He wasn't Clark Gable or James Cagney, but in the 1940s and 1950s he had starred in more than 50 Hollywood movies. A lot of them weren't very good (not really Reagan's fault – a lot of Hollywood movies of the time weren't very good).

Many Americans didn't think that an actor should be president ... and especially not Ronald Reagan. Reagan didn't really seem to know what his own politics were. He had been a Democrat and was president of the Screen Actors' Guild, a trade union, before becoming a Republican in 1962. But he got noticed by making impressive speeches and was urged to run for election as governor of California in 1966. Reagan's simple message had a wide appeal. He won the election and remained governor for eight years.

A role as real-life American football player George Gipp gave Reagan his lifelong nickname, the 'Gipper'.

Reagan promised to make 'bums' work and to stop anti-war protests at universities.

CAST LIST

- Ronald Reagan
- Nancy Reagan
- Mikhail Gorbachev

Little HISTORY

1966: Governor
1980: First term as president
1984: Second term
1989: Leaves office
1991: Fall of Soviet Union

LIGHTS!
CAMERA!
ACTION!

WARNING
IT'S ALL
AN ACT!

Keep it simple, stoopid

When Reagan ran for president in 1980, he kept it simple too. His acting experience had taught him how to communicate with an audience. He stood against the Democrat Jimmy Carter and won. Some observers were surprised – but in 1984 Reagan won again, this time by a landslide.

Positive and negative

Reagan's record as president was mixed. The United States was in a depression, and jobs were moving overseas. Some people said he didn't do enough to help the economy. In foreign affairs, though, Reagan stood up for U.S. interests. When the Soviet Union collapsed in 1991, Reagan gained a lot of credit for winning the Cold War.

Ronnie & Gorby

Reagan's political co-star was Mikhail Gorbachev, premier of the Soviet Union from 1988. Gorbachev and Reagan got on, which helped diffuse some tension of the Cold War. Gorbachev was convinced that the Soviet Union had to become more open: eventually its communist system collapsed in 1991.

TALK TO THE WORLD ...
WITH A MOUSE

We live in an 'information age' – most stuff we need to know is available through a few clicks of a computer mouse. That's all thanks to a few visionaries.

By the 1980s there were millions of computers in offices and growing numbers in homes, too. They were used for word processing or calculations, to design books, even to play games. There wasn't much that computers couldn't do ... except talk to each another. Messages were still sent by post or by fax.

One problem was that computers used loads of different programs. Another was that most were not linked. There was a system that allowed some computers in U.S. military organisations and universities to talk to each other. It was called the Internet. But it was so complex that it could only really be used by specialists.

It wasn't for e-mailing your friends to set up a play date.

You could always call on a mobile phone – but they were as big as bricks (and just as heavy).

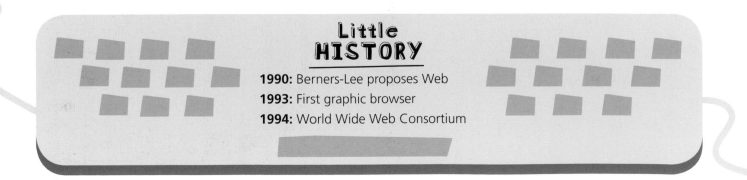

Little HISTORY

1990: Berners-Lee proposes Web
1993: First graphic browser
1994: World Wide Web Consortium

Boffin breakthrough

CERN in Switzerland – the European Organization for Nuclear Research – is home to lots of Europe's leading scientists. One of the boffins, Tim Berners-Lee, wanted to make it easier to share information, so he used an idea called HTTP (Hypertext Transfer Protocol) to allow computers to communicate easily. Now you did not have to program complex computer codes. You could just point and click on a word or picture in a file to go straight to another file, even on a different computer.

Spinning a web

In 1990 Berners-Lee and Robert Cailliau used the Internet to create the World Wide Web. They linked computers (or 'clients') to 'servers', which could store loads of information (so your computer didn't have to). Berners-Lee also invented an address system based on domain names and browsers to help find information. A graphic browser (that is, one arranged in a way that ordinary folk could use) was created in 1993 by a team at the University of Illinois.

In 1992 there were 26 servers in the world. By 2010 Google alone was thought to have more than 1 million. There were more than 235 million websites being used by 1.5 billion people. The chances are, you were one of them...

HELLO!
HELLO!

WARNING HARD DRIVE!

WHO WAS WHO?

Tim Berners-Lee (born 1955)

In 1994 Tim Berners-Lee (his friends call him TimBL) founded the World Wide Web Consortium (W3C) at Massachusetts Institute of Technology to oversee the growth of the Web. Berners-Lee also made sure that he did not copyright his idea. It was his vision that the Web should be available to everyone, so the software it used was freely available.

Hold the Front Page!

The first web page, set up at CERN, told readers how to set up web pages and browsers. It's a historical document – but no one kept a record of how it looked!

COOL WORDS

barbarians A word used by the Romans to describe the peoples who lived beyond the borders of their empire.

chivalry A system of polite values and behaviour that was promoted among knights in the Middle Ages.

civil war An armed conflict that takes place between two or more sides within a country or community.

colony An overseas settlement set up and governed by people from another country.

democracy A system of government in which people vote for representatives who make laws on their behalf.

depression A period when economic activity shrinks, creating unemployment and hardship.

empire A large area or a number of territories all ruled by the same sovereign, usually an emperor or empress.

evolution The process by which organisms change over time through a gradual series of tiny variations that allow them to adapt more closely to their environment.

independence The right of a people to govern themselves rather than be ruled by another country.

inflation A rapid rise in prices.

Middle Ages The name given to the period of European history that lies approximately between the fall of the Roman Empire in 476 and the conquest of Constantinople by the Turks in 1453.

mint To stamp metal coins; the word is also used to describe the place where coins are minted.

monastery A place where monks live lives dedicated to religious worship (the equivalent for nuns is a convent).

mummy A dead body which is preserved by being dried out and often wrapped in bandages; the Egyptians are one of a number of cultures who mummified their dead.

nomad Someone who does not have a single fixed home but who moves around, often with the seasons.

oracle A person who is believed to speak the words of a god or goddess.

pharaoh The ruler of ancient Egypt.

pilgrimage A journey made for a religious purpose, usually to pray at a shrine; all Muslims have a duty to make a pilgrimage to Mecca in Saudi Arabia at least once in their lives, if they can afford the trip.

plague A highly contagious and deadly disease; also known as the Black Death.

pyramid A structure with a square base and four sides that taper to a point at the top.

quipu Knotted strings that were used by the Inca to keep records.

Reformation A period of religious reform that began in 1517 and ended with the Protestant church splitting from the Catholic church.

Renaissance A name given to the period from roughly 1250 to roughly 1450 which saw a flowering of arts and learning throughout much of Europe, particularly Italy and the Low Countries.

revolution A period of sudden and radical change in politics or ideas; political revolution is often accompanied by violence.

sacrifice A gift made to the gods, usually of something valuable such as food, treasure or animal or human lives.

suffrage In a democracy, the right to vote.

theorem In science or maths, an idea that can be proved to be true, often as part of a bigger theory.

ziggurat A pyramid-like structure with stepped sides; also known as a step pyramid.

FIND OUT MORE

BOOKS

Adams, Simon. *Children's Atlas of World History*. London: Kingfisher Books Ltd, 2008.

Bingham, Jane. *Encyclopedia of World History*. London: Usborne, 2010.

Brocklehurst, Ruth. *The Usborne History of Britain*. London: Usborne, 2008.

Deary, Terry, and Brown, Martin. *Horrible History of the World*. London: Scholastic, 2007.

Grant, Neil. *Oxford Children's History of the World*. Oxford: OUP Oxford, 2006.

Haywood, John, et al. *Illustrated Children's Encyclopedia of the Ancient World: Step Back in Time…* London: Southwater, 2008.

King, David C. *Children's Encyclopedia of American History* (Smithsonian Institution). London: DK Publishing, 2003.

WEBSITES

http://www.bbc.co.uk/history/forkids
BBC site featuring information and games, with sections on ancient and British history, the world wars and recent history.

http://www.historyforkids.org
The Kidipede site, which contains many entries on world history and science aimed at middle school readers.

http://www.channel4learning.com/sites/essentials/history/index.shtml
4 Learning site featuring an interactive timeline from Ancient Egypt to Britain since World War II.

http://www.bbc.co.uk/schools/primaryhistory/
The BBC website for primary schools, with sections on ancient Greece and Rome, articles on children in history, an interactive timeline and a history of the world in objects.

INDEX

Africa 34–35, 68–69, 76–77
American Civil War 75
American Independence 64–65
American Revolution 60–61
Apollo program 88-89
Armstrong, Neil 89
art 44–45, 86–87
Australia 58–59
Aztec 48–49

Beecher Stowe, Harriet 74–75
Berners-Lee, Tim 93
Black Death 28–29

Caligula 16–17
China 32–33
Columbus, Christopher 46–47
computers 92–93
Conquistadors 48–49
convicts 58–59
Cortés, Hernán 48–49
Croesus 14–15

Darwin, Charles 72–73
disease 28–29, 68–69, 70–71

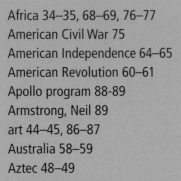

Easter Island 38–39
Egypt, ancient 10–11, 35
Eleanor of Aquitaine 22–23
England 23, 24–25, 52–53, 56
evolution, theory of 72–73
exploration 46–47, 68–69, 72–73

feudal system 28–29
France 22–23, 42–43, 57
French Revolution 57

Great Depression 84–85
Greece ancient 12–13, 18–19

Haig, Douglas 81
Hemings, Sally 65
Henry II 23

Inca 36–37
industrial revolution 66–67
Internet 92–93
Islam 34–35

Joan of Arc 42–43
John I 23, 24–25

Khan, Genghis 26–27
kingship 24–25, 56–57

Lincoln, Abraham 74–75
London 52–53, 70–71

Magna Carta 24–25
malaria 68–69
Manhattan 50–51
Mansa Musa 34–35
medicine 68–69, 70–71
Mesopotamia 8–9
Mexico 48–49
moai (statues) 38–39
money 14–15, 35
Mongols 26–27
moon 88–89
mummies 10–11

New Deal 84–85

Peru 36–37
Peter the Great 54–55
Pollock, Jackson 86–87
Pythagoras 12–13

quipu 37

Reagan, Ronald 90–91
Reformation 30–31
Renaissance 44–45
Richard the Lionheart 23
Rome, ancient 16–17
Roosevelt, Franklin D. 84–85
Russia 54–55

silk 32–33
slavery 64–65, 74–75
Snow, John 70–71
steam engines 66–67
suffragettes 82–83

taxation 60–61, 64
textiles 32–33
Try This 9, 11, 14, 17, 27, 37, 45, 54, 77, 86

Uncle Tom's Cabin 74–75
United States of America 64–65, 90–91

warfare 26–27, 42–43, 80–81
Watt, James 66–67
When the Past Was Rubbish 15, 19, 29, 33, 35, 46, 49, 53, 58, 61, 64, 70, 82, 85
Who Was Who? 12, 23, 24, 27, 34, 43, 47, 48, 51, 55, 65, 67, 68, 72, 75, 81, 85, 87, 89, 93
women's rights 82–83
World War I 80–81

CREDITS

Corbis: Louie Psihoyos/Science Fiction 72; Getty Images: Henry Guttman/Stringer 55l, The Bridgeman Art Library 87l; iStock: Travellinglight 76; MaryEvans Picture Library: 20t, 22–23t; Photolibrary: D&S Tollerton 72-73; Public Domain: 07, 19, 26, 27, 51t, 64, 71; The Library of Congress: 91; Thinkstock: iStockphoto 06t, 09, 47, Photos.com 57, 62c, 66, 74; Topfoto: The Granger Collection, New York 20c, 25, 34–35, 40c, 41, 42–43, 56–57, 78b, 83; All other photographs Shutterstock; All interior artworks Windmill Books Ltd; Cover artworks Clive Goddard.